Children's
Norfolk & Suffolk

Steve & Alyson Appleyard

Red Flannel Pu

Published in 2010 by Red Flannel Publishing

Plumtree House, Mill Lane, East Runton

Norfolk NR27 9PH

www.norfolkguides.co.uk

ISBN 978-0-9561346-1-5

Printed by Barnwell Print Ltd, Aylsham, Norfolk

Introduction

This book is our personal guide to things to do and places to visit in Norfolk and Suffolk, specifically for children. Every place to visit is a personal recommendation. Between us we have visited them all and on some visits we were accompanied by grandchildren, who gave us their views. Not every place we visited has been included in the book - inclusion has been totally our decision, no one has paid for their entry or influenced what we have said about them. We took all the photographs (with a couple of exceptions), so there is no marketing hype - it is as you see it.

We believe that together Norfolk and Suffolk are the best two counties in the country, both in terms of the number and the quality of the venues. How many others can boast so many zoos, farm parks, country parks, steam railways, museums, beaches, seaside towns, a dinosaur park, a superb theme park and the magical BeWILDerwood! If you are on holiday here - well chosen. If you live here like us - aren't we lucky. We have tried to suggest some interesting things for children to do and how to add interest to simple things like going for a walk - by turning it into a mountain climb and raising a flag when you get to the top. Yes there are mountains in Norfolk - well almost! Enjoy yourselves with your children.

Steve & Alyson Appleyard

Things to do

Places to visit

Country Parks

Railways

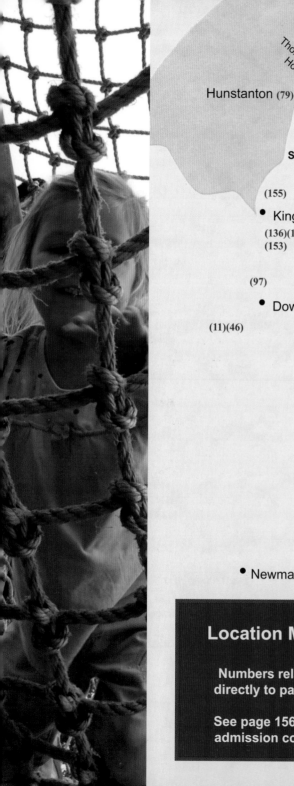

Wells-next-the-Sea (80) ●

Brancaster
Titchwell
Thornham
Holme (49)(53)

Hunstanton (79) ●

(13) (32)
(41) (42)

(42)(23)
(32)(67)
(72)(76)

(98)

Snettisham
(150)

(38)

(155)

● King's Lynn
(136)(143)
(153)

(97)

Swaffham ● (145)

● Downham Market

(11)(46)

(49)Weeting Heath
(53)(55) Brandon

Thetford ●
(30)(38)(62)
(140)

(135) West Stow
(50)Lackford Lakes
(18)

● Newmarket

Bury St Edmunds ●
(38)(57)
(149)

Location Map

**Numbers relate
directly to pages**

**See page 156 for
admission costs**

Clare ●
(57)

(33) ● Blakeney

Cley (120)(121)

(49)

(70) ● Sheringham

Holt (19) (9) (12)   E & W Runton

(43)   Cromer (81)

(60)(76) (20)(30)(37)   (17)(18)(20)

(151)   (38)(39)(43)   (35)(65)(90)

(123)   (61)(63)(95)   (127)(133)

(152)

● Fakenham   (69)   Happisburgh

(11)(46)(108)   (65)   (154)

Aylsham   (33)

(103)   (73)   (120)(147)   (32)

(100) (112)

(99)(128)   (102)   ● Wroxham (146)(38)

(113)   (69) (10)(14)(49)(64)

Dereham   (74)   (116)   (23)(24)(51)   (89)

Wymondham Norwich ●   ● Great Yarmouth (82)

(19)(20)(40)(41) (107)   (132)(138)(141)

(101)   (53)(66)(115)   (142)(144)

(124)(130)(139)   (93)

(94) Attleborough   (111)

Carlton Marshes (50) ●   Lowestoft (83)

(87)   (119) (126)

Beccles   Kessingland

(55) Knettishall   (88)

Heath

(77) Diss ●   (154)

(50) Lopham Fen   (91) Halesworth   ● Southwold (84)

(39)(17) (21)

(152)   (56)   Dunwich

(11) (52)

(75) Wetheringsett   (125)

(22)   Thorpness

(155)   (21)

(137)   (58)   ● Aldeburgh

● Stowmarket (106) (105) Wickham

Market

Needham Market   (59)   Orford

(58)(104)   (155)

(21)

Woodbridge ● (133)

(21)(152)

Ipswich ● (40)(118)

(148)

● Felixstowe (85)

(155)

8 Things to do

Here are 26 things for your children to do while they are on holiday in Norfolk and Suffolk. Many of them are free, most of them are outdoors, most involve exercise and none involve a TV screen. Not that we are against television or computer games, but this is the opportunity for children to take in the fresh and hopefully warm air of East Anglia.

Perhaps it's a bit of an exaggeration to describe the hills of north Norfolk as mountains, but we wanted to get across the point that Norfolk is not a totally flat county as many believe. It also adds a challenge and excitement to a walk to tell children that we are going to climb the highest hill in Norfolk - and to raise a Union Jack when we get to the top.

On a clear day the views from the top of all three are superb, both seaward and inland. One weekend we set two of our grandchildren the challenge of climbing the three highest peaks. The first is Incleborough Hill between East and West Runton. The second is the Beeston Bump, just to the east of Sheringham and the third is Muckleburgh Hill, between Weybourne and Kelling (just west of the Muckleburgh Collection). All three have well trodden paths, two are on National Trust land and Beeston Bump is part of the cliff top path. There isn't the space here to give you detailed instructions on finding the footpaths, we recommend that you acquire the appropriate Ordnance Survey map and then you can also teach your children map reading at the same time and perhaps even how to use a compass!

10 Pond Dipping

Our first experience of pond dipping was at an event on Ranworth Broad organised by the Norfolk Wildlife Trust on their reserve. The NWT provides nets and identification charts and their experts are on hand to help with identification and to enthuse the children about what they might find.

As the NWT literature says "Our aim is to inspire children and families about Norfolk's wildlife" and this event certainly does that. Pond dipping usually takes place on one day during the week in the summer holidays at Ranworth and on another day at their Hickling Broad reserve. We recommend that you obtain a copy of the NWT leaflet which gives details of their events and the exact location of these reserves, although they are well signed from the two broads. See page 156 for NWT contact details.

At Pensthorpe there is a safe raised dipping pond that you can use at any time when visiting this conservation centre. The nets and specimen containers are on hand by the pond (top picture).

The RSPB holds organised pond dipping days at their reserve at Minsmere (bottom picture). The dates of these and other special events for children and families at Minsmere, are listed in a booklet produced by the RSPB.

Organised dipping is also conducted at the Wildlife & Wetlands Trust at Welney.

Contact and other details for Pensthorpe, the RSPB Minsmere reserve and WWT are given on page 156.

12 Rock Pooling

There are a limited number of places on the Norfolk and Suffolk coast where there are good rock pools. Probably the best place for rock pooling is West Runton and the best time to go is when the Norfolk Wildlife Trust's experts are holding one of their organised sessions. Here we can see Nick of the NWT giving an initial informative talk to everyone and after this he helps the children identify their finds. At the end everyone gathers round, while Nick talks about some of the interesting specimens. Here he is explaining about the anatomy of a crab and yes the lobster in the bucket was actually found in a rock pool. Nick's final instruction is on how important it is to carefully return the specimens to the place where they were found, See page 156 for contact details for the Norfolk Wildlife Trust.

Other places that are good for rock pooling include East Runton and Cromer's west beach. The top picture shows children at Sea Palling where pools have formed around the man made reefs. Pools also form around groynes, those at Hunstanton and Cromer's east beach are particularly popular with children with fishing nets and buckets for their catch.

14 Bug Hunting

Not only does the Norfolk Wildlife Trust organise pond dipping at their reserves on Ranworth and Hickling broads in the summer holidays, but on another day their enthusiastic experts show the children how to find and identify bugs. They peer into the crevices of the tree bark and turn over old and rotting branches, looking for beetles and other creatures of all shapes and sizes. They are provided with identification charts and specimen trays and the organisers are always on hand to help with identification. Specimens are also collected by swishing a net through the long grasses. This activity certainly appeals to the natural curiosity of children towards creepy crawlies and they can continue with their new found skills in the garden when they go home.

Children can try on a pair of the NWT's special glasses to see the world as a bug would see it - and look scary in the process. The NWT team also shows everyone how to make a bug house from reeds. The children then make one for themselves, which they can take home and hang in the garden. See page 156 for contact information for the Norfolk Wildlife Trust.

16 Crabbing

One of the most popular seaside activities for children is crabbing from a pier or quayside. Favourite locations in Norfolk are Cromer Pier and the quaysides at Wells and Blakeney. You can use a net as shown in the top photograph opposite or a single hook or line, both are sold in the nearby shops. The best bate is fish heads but as these are not so easy to come by, most crabbers use bacon or other fatty meat. The crabs are kept in buckets but should be carefully returned to the sea afterwards (not dropped from a great height!). The bottom picture shows the crabbing competition on Cromer pier during carnival week. In this you are only allowed to use a hook and line, the difficulty being to keep the crab clinging to the bait as you lift it from the water.

The best place for crabbing in Suffolk is at Walberswick near Southwold, where they hold the British Open Crabbing Championship every year. The championships are held in August and attract more than 1000 contestants (bottom picture). The competition takes place over a 90 minute period and the winner is the person who catches the heaviest crab - in 2009 the winning specimen was $4^5/_8$ ounces. The winner of the event receives a gold medal, a silver salver and a cash prize. Runners up also get medals and cash prizes - they really do take crabbing seriously in Walberswick! For further information on the competitions at Walberswick and Cromer see the websites -

www.walberswick.ws/crabbing

www.cromercarnival.co.uk

18 Fly a kite

Given that the coastline of Norfolk and Suffolk faces the North Sea, this must make it one of the windiest in the UK and an excellent place to fly a kite. So have a go, although do avoid the parts of our coast that are nature reserves, as kites disturb nesting birds. One very good place for kite flying is the cliff top at Cromer - near the Runton Road car park. This is an official site of the Norfolk Power Kite Club, as is the beach at Gorleston (see **www.npkc.org**).

The Suffolk International Kite Festival is held in May at Rougham Airfield near Bury St Edmunds. The website of the Suffolk Kite Flyers Club gives more information about this kite festival, where you will see the most amazing kites. It also gives information about kite flying at Rougham and Needham Lake. (**www.skfc.co.uk**).

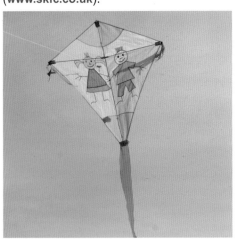

Create a puppet show 19

Within our region we are fortunate to have the unique Norwich Puppet Theatre with its 185 seat auditorium, housed in the converted medieval church of St James. They host a variety of touring puppetry companies, as well as putting on craft based workshops throughout the year (see bottom picture). On a smaller scale is the Pedlar's Barrow Puppet School at West Runton. Here you can drop in with your children and supervise them while they use their imagination to put on their own show, using the extensive range of hand puppets and costumes, (Top 2 pictures).

Norwich Puppet Theatre
www.puppettheatre.co.uk
St James, Whitefriars, Norwich
NR3 1TN   01603 629921
The Puppet School
Pedlar's Barrow, 9 Station Road
West Runton NR27 9QD 01263 837675

20 Sail a model boat

All children enjoy sailing model boats and low cost yachts are readily available from toy and gift shops. Across our region there are a number of excellent model boat ponds and the majority of them are raised for safety. The top picture shows the raised pond on the Esplanade at Sheringham.

The other two pictures of a raised pond show the slightly smaller pond in Cromer's North Park. This pond is popular during the two weeks of Cromer's carnival when there are organised events. Children are shown how to build model boats from paper and plastic cups and then they race them, creating great excitement.

The bottom left picture is the entrance to the large model boat pond at Southwold. This is not a raised pond and so children need to be closely supervised here.

Sail a model boat 21

This Thames sailing barge on the large model boat pond at Eaton Park Norwich is at the other end of the spectrum from the paper boats at Cromer. This superb model and many others made by members of the Norwich Model Boat Club can be seen regulalry at the weekend. The pavilion at the end of the pond is where the club meet. For more information about the club and when they sail see their website - **www.nmbc.fsnet.co.uk** Eaton Park is in Southpark Avenue. The popular model boating pond shown in the bottom left picture is at Aldeburgh on the seafront in Crabbe Street. The attractively situated raised pond shown bottom right is at Woodbridge. It is located in a park in the Avenue - to access it you need to take the pedestrian crossing across the railway line.

22 Row a boat at Thorpness

Thorpeness is a magical sort of place and boating on Thorpeness Meare has always been one of our favourite activities in the summer. The Meare must be one of the largest boating lakes in the country, covering some sixty acres, with lots of islands with names from Peter Pan. Despite its size the lake is safe, being never more than three feet deep. There is a wide range of boats for hire by the hour, including rowing boats, kayaks, canoes and dinghies. The Meare is open from Easter until the end of October.

Thorpeness is two miles north of Aldeburgh and was created as a holiday village in the 1920's and is little changed today. One landmark in the village is the House in the Clouds - see the middle picture - better still go and see it.

The Meare at Thorpeness is one excellent place for canoing, another picturesque lake where you can hire canoes is Abrahams Bosom at Wells-next-the-Sea (middle picture). However without doubt the best waters to really explore in a canoe are the Broads. There are large areas within the Broads that are inaccessible to motor powered boats, but which can be explored by canoe (top picture). To quote from the website of the experts -TheCanoeMan.com - "You can paddle down miles of undisturbed tributaries , dykes and streams often never seeing another soul, but often seeing the Broads best kept secrets - the Kingfishers, the Bitterns and even the elusive Otter". The bottom picture shows canoes at Salhouse Broad. See page 157 for details of canoe hire on the Broads.

24 Boating on the Broads

One of the best assets of Norfolk and Suffolk must be the Broads, which is Britain's largest protected wetland and the third largest inland waterway. There are some 190 kilometres of waterways in the region and the great thing about them is that they are lock free - unlike most other navigable inland waterways. The Broads are in effect a large number of shallow lakes (which were originally created by digging peat), connected by the rivers Bure, Ant, Thurne, Wensum, Waveney and the Yare. The 60+ broads vary in size from small pools, to the largest, the 350 acre Hickling Broad - although not all of them are connected to the rivers. The broads are for the most part less than 2m deep. Without doubt the best way to see the Broads is by boat, of which there are huge number of options to choose from.

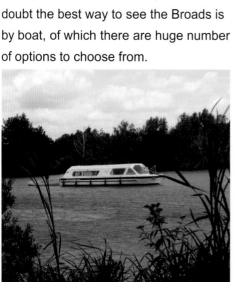

Your choice of boat could be from a small day boat which you can hire by the hour, to a ten berth motor cruiser on which you can spend a most comfortable and enjoyable holiday. You can also hire sailing boats and again you have the option of open day boats or sailing cruisers with cabins. These are all self drive options, but if you simply want to sit back and let someone else do the work, then you could take a trip on one of the large passenger cruisers. These sail from Wroxham, Potter Heigham and Horning. Alternatively you could take a trip on one of the Broads Authorities four electric boats. The top picture shows Helen which operates from Ranworth and the middle picture is of Electric Eel on the River Ant at How Hill.

Contact a Broads Authority information centre for more details. (Page 159)

26 Go camping

All children enjoy camping and our region has some great campsites. They are too numerous to mention in this book, but we can highlight four for you here. The first is Woodhill Park, a cliff top campsite overlooking the sea at East Runton and holder of a Gold award in the David Bellamy conservation scheme. (www.woodhill-park.com).The middle picture shows camping at Kelling Heath near Weybourne. Kelling is set amongst 250 acres of woodland and rare open heathland in an area of Outstanding Natural Beauty, (www.kellingheath.co.uk). The authentic Sioux style tipis are available for hire at a small campsite at Burnham Deepdale (www.deepdalefarm.co.uk). The picturesque lake with beach is part of the Moon and Sixpence campsite at Waldringfield near Woodbridge (www.moonandsixpence.eu)

Cycling is an activity that the whole family can participate in together. It provides both fun and exercise and in Norfolk and Suffolk it's not too arduous. National Cycle Network Route 1 passes through our region as does NCN 13. There is also the Norfolk Coast Cycleway NCN 30 from Great Yarmouth to King's Lynn. NCN 30 also goes from Thetford to Lowestoft. Our own preference is for traffic free routes of which there are many in the region. These include Marriott's Way, Peddars Way and Weaver's Way. The photographs here depict off road cycling in Rendlesham Forest, Thetford Forest and Kelling Heath. Information on places to hire bikes is given on page 158. For more information on routes, we recommend that you purchase one of the Goldeneye county cycle route maps.

28 Go for a hike

To say "you're going for a hike" sounds more challenging than simply going for a walk. The hike could be within one of the country parks shown in this book, or it could be one of the long distance trails that we have in our two counties. The Peddar's Way starts at Knettishall Heath and extends 46 miles to meet up with the Norfolk Coast Path near Hunstanton. This then continues a further 47 miles eastwards along the coast to Cromer. From Cromer you can continue on the Weavers Way for 56 miles to Great Yarmouth. From here you can walk the Angles Way which follows the county border westwards back to the start of the Peddars Way. We should also mention the 92 mile Suffolk Coast & Heaths path from Manningtree in Essex to Lowestoft.

Most of the nature reserves and country parks featured in this book incorporate a nature trail with information and identification boards. But why not treat every walk as a nature trail and carry identification books for wild flowers, butterflies, birds etc and of course a pair of binoculars. Teach your children - perhaps you will be learning together. Start by identifying these flowers.

30 Go on an adventure day

Most children enjoy climbing and participating in other 'dangerous' activities. We are lucky throughout our region, there are lots of parks that incorporate climbing frames and other challenging structures. We do however have two centres that specialise in this and provide activities that can really present a challenge to children, while maintaining a high level of safety.

Go on an adventure day 31

The first is the Hilltop Outdoor Centre located in 31 acres of private woodland near Sheringham. Hilltop offers adventure days for children over six years old, with bigger challenges for older children. The photographs on the facing page show children enjoying an activity based birthday party at Hilltop. Other activities here include a big zipper and high ropes, as well as archery and mountain bikes.

The second is the awesome Go Ape tree top adventure course at the High Lodge Forest Centre in Thetford Forest. Here you experience three hours of tree top adventure which includes climbing 30ft up a rope ladder, swinging Tarzan like into a giant net, zipping through the trees and crossing high wire rope bridges. The minimum age at Go Ape is ten and all under 18's must be supervised by a participating adult.

Hilltop Outdoor Centre, Old Wood,
Sheringham NR26 8TS (on the A148)
01263 824514
www.hilltopoutdoorcentre.co.uk

Go Ape at the High Lodge Forest Centre
Santon Downham IP27 0AF
Entrance off the B1107 Thetford to
Brandon road - 1 mile from Brandon.
0845 643 9146 or book online
www.goape.co.uk

32 A day on a quiet beach

The beaches of Norfolk and Suffolk are amongst the finest in the country, especially those on the North Norfolk Coast. The beach at Holkham/Wells is often voted as the best in the country and regularly features as a backdrop in photographs and films. These include the closing sequence of Shakespeare in Love and the opening shots of each episode of ITV's Kingdom. Three of our favourite quiet beaches are Brancaster (top), Winterton-on-Sea (middle) and Wells-next-the-Sea (bottom). At peak times there are many visitors on these beaches, but they are so expansive that they never appear to be over crowded. While the beaches of the east coast are not so remote, the southern parts of the beaches at Great Yarmouth, Gorleston, Southwold and Felixstowe are all invariably quiet.

Both Grey and Common seals can be seen all around our coast, often when they inquisitively raise their heads above the water. You can get a closer look at them at several locations, including islands in the Wash which appear at low water. You can reach these from Hunstanton on one of the Searles sea tours. The best known colonies are probably those at Blakeney Point, which you can visit on one of the many boats that operate from Morston (page 158). The boat operators claim that you will always see seals (top and bottom pictures). The middle picture was taken at Horsey where Grey seals give birth on the beach (to a single white pup) in November and December. At this time the beach is roped off and a viewing platform is erected so that you can observe the seals at close quarters.

34 Go swimming in the sea

Even though the North Sea can be rather cold at times, children love to swim and play around in the water when they visit any one of the many beaches in our region. We cannot stress enough that you should not let children out of your site, as our coastline can be dangerous and there have been a number of unfortunate accidents over recent years. These have been caused by rip currents which run along the coast and by turbulent currents which form around groynes. Wherever possible you should use beaches that are patrolled by lifeguards and stay between their red and yellow flags. The top picture shows Lily and Oscar enjoying the safe pools that form at Wells. For details of websites that provide information on lifeguard protected beaches and on beach safety see page 158.

While the Norfolk and Suffolk coast is not exactly Malibu, body boarding is very popular with children at beaches all around our coast. Some are beginning to progress to the more challenging activity of surfing, where they stand up on the boards - and of course fall off. It's surprising that we even have waves suitable for this, but apparently so. Five Norfolk locations actually appear on the surfing website **www.surfing-waves.com** (Cromer, East Runton, Sea Palling, Scratby and Gorleston). The Glide Surf School gives lessons at Cromer to children who are eight years and over, hiring out surf boards and wet suits when necessary.

www.glidesurfschool.co.uk
07966 392227
(Normally operates from the east beach at Cromer)

36 Fossil Hunting

Children are always fascinated by fossils and we are fortunate in having one of the best sections of coastline for finding fossils, as a result of the glacial sediments that covered our region. One particular sedimentary layer is known as the Cromer Forest Bed and can be seen at various places from Weybourne to Kessingland. The best place to see it is at the base of the cliffs at West Runton, where it presents itself as a dark band. The most famous fossil that has been found in these cliffs is the largest fossil elephant skeleton ever to have been found in Britain. The first bone from the West Runton Elephant was found by a local couple after it had become exposed following a storm in 1990 and subsequent excavations have now found the majority of the skeleton.

West Runton
Site of Special Scientific Interest

unton cliff (West Runton Freshwater bed) was deposited in a quiet river backwater.
varied fossil evidence of the plants and wildlife which lived in a period of temperate
During a much colder period, approximately 450,000 years ago, an extensive
nds and gravels which can be seen in the upper part of the cliff.

You must not dig into the cliffs at West Runton, not only is it dangerous but it is also illegal, as this section of the coast has been designated as a Site of Special Scientific Interest. You can however walk along the beach and look for the fossils that have naturally become exposed through the erosion of the cliffs by the weather and the sea. Two of the pictures here show a fossilised belemnite (a sea creature) and a piece of amber (fossilised tree sap) both of which were found locally on the beach. Nick from the Norfolk Wildlife Trust gives an excellent talk about fossils at West Runton, following his rock pooling sessions (page 12). Many fossils that have been found at West Runton have been left with Louise, the proprietor of the Seaview Beach Cafe. These include an elephant's tooth (here being held by George), a rhinoceros tooth (in Lily's hands) and on the table are two pieces of hyaena poo, which I'm sure Louise would be happy to show you. There is information about the West Runton Elephant on an information board outside the cafe and further information is provided at Cromer Museum (Page133). We can also recommend a visit to the Little Gem Rock Shop in Cromer.

38 Get lost in a maze

Children love to find their way through a maze. We have found three mazes in our region, plus several maize mazes which appear from July to September. The first of the permanent mazes is the Priory Maze and Gardens on the A149 at Beeston Regis. There is an entry charge (Admission Band B) but children can also participate in a quiz trail in the gardens. www.priorymazegardens.co.uk 01263 822986. The second permanent hedge maze is within Nowton Country Park (see page 57). The third maze is in Thetford Forest (Page 62). We have found four maize mazes but I am sure there must be more. They are - Hemsby Megamaze www.hemsbymegamaze.co.uk 01493 732307 SatNav - NR29 4NL South Creake Amazing Maize Maze www.amazingmaizemaze.co.uk 01328 823224 SatNav - NR21 9JD.

The third maize maze is on the A1059 just west of Southwold. **01379 586746** www.southwoldmaizemaze@supanet.com Most of the maize mazes have other activities for children and our favourite because it has so many extra activities, as depicted in these photographs, is The Wizard Maze at Metton near Cromer. (off the B1436) **01263 761255, NR11 8QU** www.wizardadventuremaze.co.uk

40 Try skiing & tubing

Skiing may be the last activity that you would think of in our region but we are fortunate in having two centres. The one shown in the photographs is the Norfolk Ski Club facility. Not only can children learn how to ski and snowboard here but they can have fun snow tubing. As the NSC says about snow tubing -

"..everyone can do it..great for birthday parties for all ages" (minimum age 4 years). The second ski venue is the Suffolk Ski Centre at Ipswich, which adds tobogganing to its activities - on a safe carpeted slope away from the ski slopes. Both centres are open all year.

Norfolk Ski Club - Whitlingham Lane Trowse, Norwich NR14 8TW 01603 662781 www.norfolkski.com

Suffolk Ski Centre - Bourne Hill Ipswich, IP2 8NQ 01473 602347 www.suffolkskicentre.co.uk

Go skating 41

For the past few years it has been a Christmas treat for Maisie and Zak to go ice skating on the temporary outdoor rink at the Forum in Norwich. Unfortunately it did not appear in 2009 - we understand through lack of sponsorship. Hopefully it will reappear in future years. However they can still pursue their aspiration to be as good as Torvill and Dean at either the indoor Planet Ice Rink in Norwich or at the Eco Ice Rink at the Oasis Leisure Centre in Hunstanton (bottom picture).

www.west-norfolk.gov.uk
www.ecoiceskate.com
Oasis Sports & Leisure Centre
Central Promenade, Hunstanton PE36 5BD
01485 535431 - skating open 12 - 6pm
holidays & weekends

www.planet-ice.co.uk
Planet Ice, Drayton High Road, Norwich
NR6 5DU   01603 416600
Open daily - check website for hours

42 Collect shells

The sandy beaches of North Norfolk are the best places to take children who are interested in collecting shells. In particular the beaches of Wells, Holkham, Brancaster and Thornham. The top two pictures show the beach at Thornham and the proliferation of shells on the strand line here. As we don't know a lot about shells, we thought we would consult the website of the British Shell Collectors' Club (**www.britishshellclub.org.uk**) and this has all the information you need, including a report on collecting shells on North Norfolk beaches. The shells on the tray shown below were all collected on Norfolk beaches and are on display in The Shell Museum in the small picturesque Norfolk village of Glandford. This was built in 1915 to house the shell collection of Sir Alfred Jodrell.

COLLECTING SEASHELLS
All of these seashells were collected at N...

The top picture shows part of the interior of The Shell Museum at Glandford and the middle image shows part of the enormous collection of shells which originate from all over the world. Children who are enchanted by shells should also be taken to the Peter Coke Shell Gallery in Sheringham. Here there are almost 200 shell-art creations by Peter Coke, a well known actor who lived at Sharrington Hall and died in 2008 at the age of 95.

The Shell Museum
Glandford (Near Holt) NR25 7JR
01263 740081 www.shellmuseum.org.uk
Opens Easter Saturday until end October
10.00 to 12.30 & 14.00 to 16.30
Closed Sunday & Monday
Admission Band A
The Shell Gallery
Off West Promenade, Sheringham
Opens Easter to end of September
12.00 to 16.00 Wednesday - Saturday
Admission free but do give a donation

44 Bird Watching

Norfolk and Suffolk are two of the best counties for watching birds. Here we have a wide range of habitats, from the coastal areas of the east and the north, through the Broads and the Fens to the Brecks in the west. We are fortunate in having a huge number of reserves, managed by organisations who all encourage children to pursue an interest in bird watching. So while you are in our region, see if you can see an Avocet, a Bittern or a Kingfisher.

The first place to encourage children to observe and identify birds is in your own garden. No matter where you live or how small your garden, you will already have birds visiting, but you can encourage more by putting out food and water. This may be in the form of nut and seed feeders as here, or home made fat feeders or food scraps. Even though binoculars are not essential in the garden, it's good to start children using them, as they need to practice holding them steady and getting the birds into view. Encourage children to identify birds for themselves, by noting their key characteristics and then looking them up in a book such as the RSPB Children's Guide to Bird Watching. Let them take part in the RSPB's annual Big Garden Birdwatch each year, not only will you be helping with this annual census, but if you keep your records from one year to the next you can monitor how successful you have been in attracting birds to your garden. If you have a digital camera let your children learn to take photographs. These pictures of a Greater Spotted Woodpecker and a Gold Finch were taken through our kitchen window with the simplest of digital cameras. The feeders are less than two metres from the window!

46 Bird watching at Pensthorpe

For your first birding excursion with your children, we highly recommend a day at Pensthorpe Conservation Centre. This is the venue for the BBC's Springwatch programme which has done so much to popularise the observation of bird behaviour. The feature of Pensthorpe is that not only are there lots of birds, but you can get really close to them inside huge walk through aviaries, where natural habitats have been created. This photograph of a Lapwing and the Avocet on page 44, were taken inside one of the aviaries, without the need of a zoom lens. Beyond the aviaries Pensthorpe is huge, with lakes, gardens, hides and above all lots of birds. There is always much to see at Pensthorpe throughout the year, including floodlit feeding from October to February (See also Pages 108 and 109).

Bird watching at Welney 47

Another recommended visit to enthuse children about birds is to the Welney Wetland Centre. A visit in the winter is particularly spectacular when you can sit in a centrally heated observatory and watch up to 9000 Whooper and Bewick's Swans join thousands of migratory ducks and other water birds from their Arctic breeding grounds. Make sure you are there at 3.30pm when the swans are fed - a unique sight. There is something different to see each season at this Wildfowl & Wetlands Trust venue and it also has a very informative visitor centre with a permanent Fenland exhibition area. There are informative display boards about swan migration in the observatory.

www.wwt.org.uk/welney
Hundred Foot Bank, Welney PE14 9TN
01353 860711 Open 7 days a week
Admission Band C

48 Bird watching with the NWT

If you live in Norfolk we can highly recommend joining the Norfolk Wildlife Trust. The NWT look after some thirty nature reserves across the county, five of which have visitor centres. If you are holidaying in the area then do visit the nearest reserve and centre. Children can become involved in the Wildlife Watch Club through which the NWT organise watch activities aimed at children 7 -12 years old (although younger children are also welcome). As the NWT say on their website - "Explore the amazing world of wildlife and discover ways in which you can help animals throughout the year. Learn how to send in your wildlife sightings and look out for the secret signs that birds, animals and bugs leave behind". There are also some fun wildlife games on the NWT website.

The five NWT visitor centres are at -
Cley Marshes This award winning visitor centre is at one of the UK's best bird watching sites. The centre has informative audio-visual presentations and a telescope overlooking the reserve - see the pictures on the opposite page. Entry to the centre is free, there is a small charge for access to the reserve (Children and NWT members are free).
Ranworth Broad This floating thatched visitor centre, which is accessed by a boardwalk and overlooks the broad, has very good hands-on learning activities. George and Lily particularly enjoyed handling the items on the touch table. Entry is free but do give a donation.
Holme Dunes This centre is located in a house on the reserve which forms part of the Norfolk Coast Area of Outstanding Natural Beauty (bottom picture).
Hickling Broad This centre is based on the largest Norfolk Broad where you can see Bitterns, Cranes and Marsh Harriers. Electric powered boat trips take you to see wildlife on the broad.
Weeting Heath A popular attraction at this reserve are the Stone Curlews, but also look out for Woodlark and Tree Pipits as well as the rare Breckland flora.
For NWT contact information - page 156

50 Bird watching with the SWT

If you are fortunate enough to live in Suffolk, then we highly recommend that you join the Suffolk Wildlife Trust who own or manage some fifty reserves and have a very active education program and around a dozen Wildlife Watch groups. The Wildlife Watch groups which are aimed at 6-12 year old children meet once a month at a weekend.

If you are just visiting the county then try to visit at least one of the reserves, they are all free to visit. There is not enough space to list them all here, but we can mention two that have visitor centres. These are -

Lackford Lakes - 121 hectares of wetland, woodland, scrub and sandy heath, designated a Site of Special Scientific Interest. The visitor centre offers stunning views across the reserve (top two photographs).

Redgrave & Lopham Fen National Nature Reserve is the largest valley fen in England (162 hectares) and is one of the most important wetlands in Europe. It is the source of the River Waveney. We can also mention the **Carlton Marshes** reserve near Lowestoft which has an education centre and runs a very grood program for school visits.

See page 156 for contact information.

Bird watching at How Hill 51

The Broads offers one of the best opportunities for bird watching. Here you have the chance to see and hear a wide range of birds, including the elusive Bittern and one of our favourites, the Kingfisher. We made a memorable trip from How Hill Staithe on 'Electric Eel', one of the Broads Authority electric powered boats. We glided silently along narrow dykes and then walked a short distance to a hide, from where we were able to observe Kingfishers - our expert guide knew exactly where to find them. This trip lasts for 50 minutes and it is advisable to book as the boat only takes six people. It is not suitable for children under two. It leaves every hour on the hour, daily June to September and at Easter and half term. At weekends April, May and October. To book call 01692 678763.

52 Bird watching with the RSPB

The RSPB is our leading national organisation for birds and it is well worth becoming a member, particularly if you wish to develop your children's interest in birds. Your children can become RSPB Wildlife Explorers and receive regular magazines with information and activities appropriate for under twelves. From thirteen years old, children become members of RSPB Phoenix, which provides them with information and activities for teenagers. Children can earn bronze, silver and gold Wildlife action awards by carrying out specific activities. The RSPB website also has very good information and games for children. There are thirteen RSPB reserves in Norfolk and Suffolk, the four with visitor centres are listed here.

Minsmere reserve is on the Suffolk coast just south of Dunwich. Nature trails take you through a variety of habitats to hides and also to the beach. The scrape at Minsmere hosts a large colony of Avocets. Minsmere also holds a sizeable proportion of the UK population of Bitterns. There are events all year round. Family explorer backpacks and trail booklets are available. The pictures on this page were taken at Minsmere.

Bird watching with the RSPB 53

Titchwell Marsh reserve is on the North Norfolk coast east of Hunstanton. Around the visitor centre are lots of feeders with a viewing area and bird recognition boards. This gave George and Lily an opportunity to learn to look through their binoculars and telescope and to identify the various birds that were feeding here. There is a mile long walk down to the sandy beach. This takes you past reed beds and shallow lagoons that are usually full of birds. **Lakenheath Fen** near Brandon is a large wetland that was converted from arable farmland and here it is possible to see Cranes and Golden Oriole. **Strumpshaw Fen** south of Norwich has reed beds, woodlands, and orchid rich meadows where you can see Barn Owls and Kingfishers.

See page 156 for contact information.

54 Country Parks

In this section we give you a selection of the many well managed open spaces that you can find in our region. We have highlighted the child friendly features of each, but there is always something for the whole family. For instance if you visit the National Trust's Sheringham Country Park in June, you will be rewarded with a spectacular display of rhododendrons.

Brandon Country Park

This park was originally parkland associated with a country house. The lake has extensive wildlife and the forest paths are ideal for gentle rambles where you may see deer. It has a visitor centre with cafe. There is an extensive programme of organised activities throughout the year, such as a children's treasure trail, nest box workshop and pond dipping. It is on the B1106 between the A11 and Brandon.

Knettishall Heath Country Park

Knettishall is a mixture of open heathland, riverside meadow and mixed woodland. There are four marked trails and the long distance paths - Peddars Way, Icknield Way and Angles Way all pass through Knettishall. There is a round the year programme of events including treasure trails, fungi walks and Santa's grotto. Knettishall is 6 miles east of Thetford, signed from the A1066 and B1111 in Barningham.

56 Dunwich Heath

Dunwich Heath is a beautiful stretch of the Suffolk coast within an 'Area of Outstanding Natural Beauty', owned by the National Trust. The heath is covered by magnificent pink and purple flowering heather from late June until September. There are three waymarked trails. A children's trail and children's tracker packs can be purchased from the shop. Within the old coastguard building is a shop, a cafe and a lookout.

Organised events at Dunwich Heath include a Great Egg Hunt (at Easter), Family Fun-Have-A-Go days in August, (for children up to 12) Halloween on the Heath, and Search For Santa.

Location - 1 mile south of Dunwich, signed from the A12 at Yoxford and Blythburgh. Telephone 01728 648501
www.nationaltrust.org.uk

Clare Castle Country Park

Clare Castle Country Park, which is only two minutes walk from the market square, contains the remains of a 13th century stone castle keep. Also within the park is the former Clare railway station and goods yard. The old goods shed now houses historical displays. A nature trail with information boards takes in the River Stour and the Railway Walk. There are various children's events, see - **www.suffolk.gov.uk**

Nowton Country Park

This country park is off the A134 south of Bury St. Edmunds (SatNav IP29 5LU). It has a ranger centre, an impressive avenue of lime trees, a bird feeding area, a pond, a totem pole, a play area, a wildflower meadow and a maze made from 2500 hornbeam trees which have created over two miles of hedging. The Nowton Park Country Fair is held on the third Sunday in June. **www.stedmundsbury.gov.uk**

58 Tunstall Forest

Tunstall Forest is located in the Suffolk coastal belt known as the Sandlings. It is a popular area for walkers, cyclists and horesriders and a motor cycle event is held twice yearly. There are both wooded and heathland areas where you can see ground nesting birds such as the Nightjar and Woodlark. The forest is due east of the A12 at Wickham Market on the B1078. The Sandgalls picnic site is off the B1069.

Needham Lake

Needham Lake is a small nature reserve and picnic area. A walk around the lake takes about 20-30 minutes and other paths allow visitors to explore further along the River Gipping. There are picnic and play areas. Fishing requires a permit which can be obtained from Bosmere Tackle in Needham Market. Needham Lake is off the B1113 south of Needham Market.

www.midsuffolk.gov.uk

Rendlesham Forest is where the UK's most significant UFO event took place in 1980. A group of American airmen from the US airbase that surrounds the forest, were reportedly confronted one night with an alien spaceship which came down over the trees and landed in a blinding explosion of light. This has inspired the building of the 'Out of This World' play area, comprising wooden play structures with names like Crashed Bomber and UFO Landing Zone. There is also an interesting maze (bottom right). There are several trails including the 3 mile UFO trail, which visits some of the significant areas connected to the sighting. Rendlesham Forest is excellent for cycling, a leaflet showing the trails is available from the forest office. Take the B1084 Woodbridge to Orford road.

www.forestry.gov.uk

60 Holt Country Park

Holt Country Park extends to some 100 acres of mainly woodland, containing more than 30 species of trees. Access has been thoughtfully planned with a system of broad rides, woodland glades and waymarked walks. One of the routes is designed for the less mobile, or for families with push chairs. Throughout the park there are interesting features such as a totem pole, carved stile, play area, viewing tower and a wooden xylophone (bottom right).

There is a visitor centre with shop, an orienteering course, a marked cycle route and an attractive pond. There are lots of organised events throughout the year. George and Lily made these swords and shields at a medieval event. Holt Country Park is on the B1149 just south of Holt. **www.northnorfolk.org**

Sheringham Country Park 61

This is a large landscaped park created in 1812 and now owned by the National Trust. There are miles of waymarked walks, many suitable for wheelchairs and push chairs. There are several viewing towers, some give spectacular views over the rhododendrons and azaleas and the highest, which is above the tree tops, gives magnificent views along the coast.

There is a visitor centre and lots of organised activities throughout the year, including family picnic days, Easter egg trail, and Wild Child events such as Big Bug Hunt, Batty Bats, Mad Moths and Spooky Halloween Trail. There is a new area to make artistic creations from irregular shaped pieces of wood. The park is 5 miles west of Cromer on the A148. **www.wild-child.org.uk**

www.nationaltrust.org.uk/sheringham

62 Thetford Forest

Thetford Forest is Britain's largest lowland pine forest and offers lots of recreational activities. The High Lodge Centre is where many of the activities are based, including an adventure play area (also Go Ape, page 31) and a giant play sculpture trail which leads to the Squirrels Maze. This is in the shape of a pine cone and is created using pine trees. There are miles of excellent off-road cycling trails, ranging from family friendly to more challenging black routes. Bikes can be hired from Bike Art who are based at the centre (see page 157). Thetford Forest is of course perfect for walking, with some 26 different trails. There are other picnic areas in the forest such as Lynford Stag on the A134. High Lodge is located off the B1107 Thetford to Brandon road. **www.forestry.gov.uk/thetfordforestpark**

Kelling Heath is set amongst 250 acres of woodland and rare open heathland, just south of the coastal village of Weybourne. Kelling Heath employs a countryside team who manage the estate and have developed a number of nature trails and woodland walks. Self guided leaflets on the trails are available for a small charge from the park reception. There are also marked cycle routes for cyclists of all abilities (see page 27). Car parking is provided from where you can start the trails, or you can walk from the North Norfolk Railway's Weybourne station or Kelling Heath's own halt, a request stop with access directly to the park. Kelling Heath has a captive Red Squirrel breeding programme.

Contact information - 01263 588181

www.kellingheath.co.uk

64 Fairhaven

The Fairhaven Woodland and Water Garden is set in 130 acres of ancient woodland with its own private broad. It has three miles of quiet woodland paths and a children's nature trail. There are boat trips on the broad from April to October. Open daily (Except Christmas day). There is a tearoom. Admission cost is band B. Fairhaven is at South Walsham.
(SatNav NR13 6DZ) **www.fairhaven.co.uk**

Salhouse Broad

Salhouse Broad is unique in having a shelving beach to the water. You can access it either by boat or by car - the car park is off the road eastwards out of Salhouse village. There is a circular walk, a picnic and rustic play area. Canoes can be hired - (bottom picture on page 23 & page 157). A water taxi to the Hoveton Great Broad Nature Trail is available in Spring and Summer. **www.salhousebroad.org.uk**

Felbrigg Hall Park 65

The woodland and parkland around the National Trust's Felbrigg Hall is one of our favourite places for walking. There are several marked trails to follow. There are a number of events specifically for children throughout the year, including Busy Bee Workshops, Teddy Bears' Picnic and Halloween Trail. There is a gift shop, cafe and restaurant. Felbrigg is on the B1436 west of Cromer. SatNav NR11 8PR.

Blickling Hall Park

Blickling is one of England's great Jacobean houses and the lake and parkland around it offer numerous opportunities for interesting walks, including a part of Weavers' Way. The walks incorporate information boards. There are usually many special events during the year such as an Easter Trail, Jolly the Jester, Go Wild at Blickling and Clowning Around. Location - $1\frac{1}{2}$ miles NW of Aylsham.

66 Whitlingham Country Park

Whitlingham Country Park which is just south of Norwich, is centred around two broads close to the River Yare, although there is no boat access to the broads from the river. There are footpaths and cycle paths around the larger Great Broad and through Whitlingham Woods. There is a visitor centre with cafe and the Whitlingham Outdoor Education Centre is located at the end of Great Broad. This offers courses or just single sessions of activities, including sailing, windsurfing, canoeing, archery, climbing and off road biking. You can visit the park using the river bus from Norwich city centre (Easter to end September). www.cityboats.co.uk

www.whitlinghamoec.co.uk
Whitlingham Lane, Trowse, Norwich
NR14 8TR 01603 632307

Holkham National Nature Reserve 67

As the Holkham website says - "This is the most extensive, diverse and dramatic nature reserve on a coastline famous for nature reserves". The Holkham Reserve covers some 4,000 hectares, stretching from Burnham Norton to Blakeney. The core section of the reserve is from Wells to Holkham Bay, which is crisscrossed by paths. The main feature of the reserve here is the pinewood, which faces the vast expanse of beach. On the landward side of the pine trees can be seen warblers, such as Lesser Whitethroat and Blackcap. On the seaward side are wading birds and the sand dunes which provide important nesting areas for shore birds . This part of the Holkham nature reserve can be accessed off the A149 three miles west of Wells-next-the-Sea.

www.holkham.co.uk/naturereserve

68 Railways

All children enjoy a train journey and in Norfolk and Suffolk we have everything, from full size steam engines and vintage carriages, to the longest $10\frac{1}{4}$" narrow gauge steam railway in the world. Do check out the special events for the railway near you - including Santa Specials in December.

The Bittern Line 69

While this section of the book is about the various heritage and narrow gauge railways to be found in our region, for those who enjoy travelling by train you may wish to consider a journey on the Bittern Line from Norwich to Sheringham. In an article in the *Independent*, Anthony Lambert included the Bittern Line in his list of the 50 best rail journeys in the world - alongside the Rocky Mountains and the Orient Express! Although even as a keen advocate of Norfolk, I'm not sure I would put the Bittern Line in this league! It stops at Salhouse and Wroxham (on the Broads), Worstead, North Walsham, Gunton, Roughton Road, Cromer, West Runton and then finally Sheringham. You could at least try the Cromer to Sheringham section which runs along the coast and takes just eight minutes.

70 North Norfolk Railway

The North Norfolk Railway operates on a five mile line between the towns of Sheringham and Holt. It is also known as the Poppy Line and was once part of the Midland & Great Northern Joint Railway network. The line closed in 1964 but was re-opened in stages from 1976 by enthusiasts and today is one of Britain's foremost heritage railways, carrying over 126,000 passengers a year. The railway operates to a published timetable all year round, but not every day in the winter.

They have a number of steam and diesel locomotives in service and others undergoing restoration. You can see the full list on the NNR website. They also have some interesting rolling stock, including newly restored vintage coaches.

Between Sheringham and Holt, trains stop at a station in the coastal village of Weybourne and at a platform within Kelling Heath. As well as the regular service there are numerous special days, some just for children and others of interest to the whole family.

'Altogether Now' are weekends when children have an opportunity to see behind the scenes and find out how the railway works. On another weekend there is an annual vintage transport festival, when classic cars, trucks and motorcycles congregate at Holt station. A 1940's weekend is considered to be one of the best re-enactment events in the country. Of course the Santa Specials need no explanation - you join the train at Sheringham to meet Santa in his grotto at Weybourne station.

www.nnrailway.co.uk

72 Wells & Walsingham Railway

The Wells & Walsingham Light Railway is claimed to be the longest $10^{1}/_{4}$" narrow gauge steam railway in the world. It operates a regular service from Wells-next-the-Sea to the picturesque pilgrimage town of Walsingham, a distance of four miles. The journey through scenic Norfolk countryside passes under five bridges and stops at Wareham St. Mary and Wighton. The station at Walsingham is close to the centre which you can explore before catching a later train back. The main engine is a unique Garratt steam locomotive built in 1986 especially for the line. The station at Wells, which is a restored signal box, is on the A149 just to the east of the town. The railway usually operates from Easter to the end of October. Tel 01328 711630.

www.wellswalsinghamrailway.co.uk

Bure Valley Railway 73

The Bure Valley Railway operates on a fifteen inch gauge line between the market town of Aylsham and Wroxham the 'capital' of the Norfolk Broads, a distance of nine miles. It follows the course of the River Bure, stopping at the villages of Brampton, Buxton and Coltishall. It has an impressive range of steam and diesel locomotives and rolling stock. The station at Aylsham has a well stocked souvenir and model railway shop, a cafe and an engine workshop that you can occasionally peer inside. A daily service operates from May to September and in half term holidays and most weekends in the year. Special events include, Teddy Bear Express, Easter Eggspress, Mothers VIP day, Spooky Express and Santa Specials. SatNav Aylsham - NR11 6BW Wroxham - NR12 8UU www.bvrw.co.uk

74 Mid-Norfolk Railway

The Mid-Norfolk railway runs between Dereham and Wymondham along eleven miles of restored track. Most of the trains are heritage diesel railcars that would have operated on rural branch lines in the 1960's. The one shown in the pictures has been beautifully restored by the enthusiasts who run this railway. They also have three Class 31 heritage diesel locomotives - these can usually be seen at Dereham station (Station Road NR19 1DF), which also has a cafe and a small museum. The station at Wymondham is in Becketswell Road (not to be confused with the mainline station). The service generally operates during weekends and some Wednedays and Thursdays from April to October, plus Santa Specials.

Tel - 01362 690633   **www.mnr.org.uk**

Mid-Suffolk Light Railway Museum 75

A group of enthusiasts has restored the small Brockford Station at Wetheringsett and a short section of the old branch line that closed in 1952. There is a collection of rolling stock - including passenger carriages dating from the 19th century. Steam trains operate on selected days during the year as part of themed events such as Middy at War, Vintage Buses and Rail 'n' Road. There is also a permanent exhibition room which is home to a collection of artefacts, documents and models. There is a shop and refreshment room. The museum is open between 11am and 5pm on Sundays and Bank Holidays, from Easter until the end of September, plus Sundays in December for Santa Specials. Brockford Station is off the A140 at Wetheringsett IP14 5PW
01449 766899   **www.mslr.org.uk**

76 Wells Harbour Railway

The Wells Harbour Railway is a $10^1/_4$" gauge railway running for approximately one mile alongside Beach Road from the town to the Pinewoods Holiday Park. The Pinewoods station is also adjacent to the Abraham's Bosom boating lake and the superb Wells beach. The railway generally operates from Easter to the October half term. SatNav NR23 1DR for the Harbour Station.

Holt Station

The North Norfolk Railway's Holt station has a number of attractions making it worthy of a visit in its own right. There is the William Marriott Railway Museum, a 00 gauge model railway, and a 280m long raised track of dual 3.5" and 5" gauge. The latter, which gives rides on specific days, is operated by the North Norfolk Model Engineering Club. Holt station is just off the A148 east of Holt. www.nnrailway.co.uk

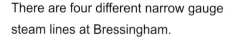

There are four different narrow gauge steam lines at Bressingham.

The **Nursery Railway** is a 2.5 mile 2ft track which gives views of the nursery of Bressingham gardens. The **Garden Railway** is 1,200m of $10\frac{1}{4}$" gauge track. The **Waveney Valley Railway** is 15" gauge and runs over low lying water meadows and through banks of rhododendrons. The **Standard Gauge** line usually operates on Sundays and special event days. There is also a display of static engines in a shed. Bressingham has many other attractions, including a Dad's Army recreation and one of the finest three abreast Gallopers.

www.bressingham.co.uk
IP22 2AA 01379 686903
2.5 miles west of Diss on A1066
Admission Band F (includes rides)

78 The Seaside

Norfolk and Suffolk together has over 130 miles of coastline with more than 50 miles of superb beaches and numerous coastal towns and villages. Our region is renowned as a seaside holiday destination. Here we have selected six destinations where you can have a 'traditional' children's seaside holiday. We apologise in advance to Sheringham and Aldeburgh and the other excellent seaside towns that we have omitted to include.

Hunstanton 79

Hunstanton is one of our most popular seaside destinations, partly because it is the most westerly and so it is the closest for those heading to the coast from inland towns. It is also popular because it has everything that a seaside town should have, including pony rides on the beach (the only place which we could find in our region). It has fun rides along the promenade, a Sea Life Sanctuary that has an impressive aquarium, boat trips to see the seals, a sports and leisure centre with indoor swimming pool and eco friendly ice rink, and of course an excellent beach. There is the Pier Family Entertainment Centre with amusements and bowling - but alas no pier. Hunstanton has well tended gardens and a large green, which make it an attractive seaside town.

80 Wells-next-the-Sea

Wells has been described as "an unspoiled seaside destination waiting to be discovered" - although lots of people have discovered it, as the car parks are usually full in the summer. Many are attracted by what is probably the best beach along the whole of the east coast. The town and its quay are almost one mile up an estuary from the sea and beach. It is still a working fishing port and the quay is popular for crabbing. Shops and restaurants line the quay and the small town stretches back from here. A small railway takes you to the beach, past a pitch and putt golf course. Near to the beach is an outdoor leisure area known as Abraham's Bosom with a large boating lake and trampolines. Some of the attractive wooden beach huts can be hired from Pinewoods Holiday Park.

www.pinewoods.co.uk

Cromer is described as the "Gem of the Norfolk Coast" and it is certainly an unspoilt traditional small seaside town. It is very much a destination for families with young children, the fun fair area located on the promenade has young children's rides. A big attraction at Cromer is its carnival in August, not only is the carnival day itself a great event, but there are two weeks of organised events for children on the beach and promenade (**www.cromercarnival.co.uk**). A permanent feature of Cromer is its pier, there to simply walk along, to crab from (page 16) or to watch the traditional seaside show. Most children are happy to spend much of their time on the beach, this can be enhanced by hiring a beach chalet for a week from the District Council. 01263 516067

www.north-norfolk.gov.uk

82 Great Yarmouth

Great Yarmouth is recognised as one of the top seaside holiday destinations in the country. The main attraction is the Pleasure Beach fun park, which occupies a nine acre seafront location and attracts some 1.5 million visitors. It has over 20 large rides, including the Sky Drop, the Log Flume and a Roller Coaster built in 1933. One of the newer attractions is a big wheel, which takes you up 34 metres in a glass capsule. Other attractions along Marine Parade include, the Merrivale Model Village, the Sea Life Centre and the Amazonia Reptillium. Great Yarmouth has several excellent museums (see the museums section). It would be easy to forget to mention the beach, as much of it is hidden behind the seafront attractions, but we will mention it as it is such an exceptionally fine beach.

Lowestoft is located on the most easterly point of the British coast and conjures up "fishing port" for many, although it is very much a seaside holiday destination. We visited Lowestoft on a warm sunny day in August, when many holiday makers were having fun on the fine beach. Others were enjoying the organised entertainment in the small park nearby. A reminder of the heyday of the fishing industry is the trawler Mincarlo, which is moored in the yacht harbour and is often open to the public. Away from the seafront but still within Lowestoft is Nicholas Everitt Park, which sits alongside Oulton Broad. There are a number of attractions for children here, including a children's play area, crazy golf and a small boating lake with canoes. Your stay in Lowestoft could be enhanced with the hire of a beach hut.

84 Southwold

Southwold is a delightful and unspoilt seaside town and if you have never been there you should put it high on your list of places to visit. At the northern end of the seafront is a large model boat pond and a boating lake with paddle boats. The boating lake is overlooked by a tearoom, where you can sit while watching your children go round in circles. At the southern end is the harbour on the River Blythe, where you can buy fresh fish and excellent fish and chips. The pier has been completely restored in the last few years and has shops and cafes in keeping with Southwold. It also has a whacky amusement arcade called "Under the pier show" designed by Tim Hunkin (**www.underthepier.com**).
Beach huts can be hired by the day or week.

Having only ever thought of Felixstowe as a container port, I was amazed when I first visited the town to find that it is a large seaside town comparable with the best. It is described as the "Garden resort of the East Coast" and the northern end of the four miles long seafront has the very attractive Spa Gardens. A promenade extends the whole length of the seafront, along which there are children's rides and amusements. At the most southerly end of the beach it becomes a Suffolk Wildlife Trust nature reserve. From here the ships appear huge as they enter the River Orwell, but the container port is out of site and does not impinge on the town. The Spa Theatre offers holiday entertainment and the leisure centre near the seafront has a swimming pool.

86 Exotic Animals

It doesn't need us to tell you that children love to visit the zoo and in our region we are spoilt for choice. Having visited them all, we can say that they are all excellent zoos, providing the maximum amount of space and the very best of conditions for their animals.

Banham Zoo 87

Banham Zoo was the winner of the EDP Berry Savory award for best large visitor attraction in both 2007 and 2008. Deservedly so, as it is undoubtedly one of the best zoos in the country. It is large and spacious and all the animals have plenty of space, particularly the giraffes - which you can view from the 'Zarafa Heights' walkway. New for 2009 was the 'Province of the Snow Cat' enclosure, which allows you to get up close to the snow leopard - pictured opposite. Other favourites include the Fur seals, the tigers and the penguins. Banham Zoo has all the facilities that you would expect, including cafes and a road train.

www.banhamzoo.co.uk
The Grove, Banham, NR16 2HE
Signed from A11 and A140 01953 887771
Open 7 days a week except -
Christmas Day and Boxing Day
Admission Band F

88 Africa Alive

The aim of Africa Alive is to recreate the African Savannah, where the animals roam freely together as in the wild. The owners have certainly succeeded in creating one of the UK's best wildlife attractions at Kessingland - within 100 acres of coastal parkland. My particular favourites were the rhinos and the next time I visit I will take the Land Rover trip into the enclosure. As well as the African animals there is farmyard corner, where children can feed and stroke domestic animals. Other attractions include the hands on Discovery Centre, indoor and outdoor adventure play areas, and the safari road train.

www.africa-alive.co.uk
White's Lane, Kessingland, NR33 7TF
On A12, 3 miles south of Lowestoft
Open 7 days a week except -
Christmas Day and Boxing Day
01502 740291 Admission Band F

89 Thrigby Hall Wildlife Gardens

One of the most popular attractions at Thrigby Hall is the tiger enclosure, which is constructed in such a way that you can meet them at treetop level. It is as if the tigers are free and the visitors are caged. There has been some commendable work carried out here on tiger conservation. The swamp house is another unusual feature of Thrigby Hall, allowing you to see crocodiles and alligators at close quarters. There is a walk through aviary which has a large selection of unusual birds. There is also a large number of waterfowl on the lake and around the attractive gardens - and much more to see here.

www.thrigbyhall.co.uk
Thrigby Hall, Filby, NR29 3DR
SatNav - Set for City Centre, Thrigby
Signed from A47 at Acle
01493 369477 Open 7 days a week
Admission Band E

90 Amazona Zoo

Amazona Zoo at Cromer opened relatively recently and is already becoming a popular place to visit. It occupies a ten acre site within walking distance of Cromer town centre. A feature of the zoo is the lake, with one area being home to Chilean flamingos. An island within the lake is home to Spider monkeys. The water within Amazona Hall contains Red-tailed catfish and Red-bellied piranha. Also in this part of the zoo are iguanas, an anaconda and a boa. There is a feline forest with puma, jaguar and ocelot. There is a large play area, a cafe and picnic tables.

www.amazonazoo.co.uk
Hall Road, Cromer NR27 9JG
Signed Zoo Park from Cromer centre.
01263 510741
Open daily 1 April - 1 November
Admission Band E

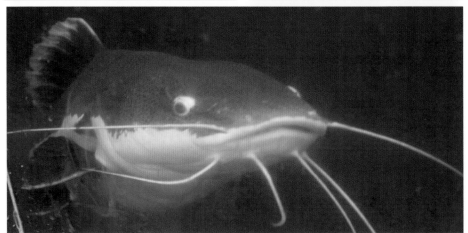

Oasis Camel Centre

A camel centre is perhaps the last thing you would expect to find in a quiet part of Suffolk, but we can assure you that there is one and it is well worth a visit. It is not just the home of camels, but other 'camelids' - llamas, alpacas and guanacos. There is a barn where they hold petting sessions with rabbits, guinea pigs and ferrets and paddocks with domestic farm animals. But it is the camels that are the focus and the 'meet the camel' talks are the highlight. Children can stroke a camel, have a photograph taken and learn all about camels. There is a land train ride around the centre and a children's play area.

www.oasiscamelcentre.co.uk
Orchard Farm, Cratfield Road, Linstead,
IP19 0DT 07836 734748
Adjacent to B1123 6 miles from Halesworth
Open daily Easter to end October
Admission Band D

92 Horses

If your children like horses then these three sanctuaries are delightful places to take them. All three do extremely commendable work in terms of animal welfare and deserve our support, so do visit them if you are in the area.

Redwings 93

Redwings have three horse sanctuaries in the UK. They have centres in Essex and Warwickshire as well as this one in Norfolk. Their prime objective is to provide a caring permanent home for horses, ponies, donkeys and mules in need. The Caldecott Visitor centre has over seventy acres of paddocks, which you can walk around and meet the rescued horses and donkeys. There are tractor rides, walking tours and horse care demonstrations. The Horse Wise Education Centre has informative and interactive displays. There is a cafe and a children's play area. Family fun days are held at each centre twice a year.

www.redwings.co.uk
Caldecott Visitor Centre NR31 9EY
On A143 Between Gt Yarmouth & Beccles
Open daily Easter to end October
Admission Free - but do give a donation
0870 040 0033

94 World Horse Welfare Hall Farm

World Horse Welfare was previously known as ILPH (International League for the Protection of Horses). They have four centres throughout the UK including Hall Farm at Snetterton. Hall Farm is home to around 120 rescued horses and ponies. There are up to four miles of walks around the paddocks, most of which are pushchair friendly and tractor and trailer rides also operate. There is an informative visitor centre, an excellent cafe, extensive picnic areas and a children's play area. There are special events organised throughout the year - check the website for details.

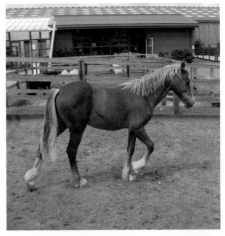

www.worldhorsewelfare.org
*Hall Farm, Ada Cole Avenue, Snetterton
NR16 2LR 01953 499100 - Close to A11
Open all year on Wednesdays, weekends
and Bank Holidays
Admission Free - but do give a donation
0870 040 0033*

Hillside Animal Sanctuary

The Hillside Animal Sanctuary in West Runton was previously known as the Shire Horse Centre. It now campaigns on behalf of all farm animals and has more than a thousand rescued animals at Hillside - as well as the original Shire horses. It also campaigns against intensive and factoring farming and much of the displayed information relates to this. There is a large collection of farming bygones, carts, wagons, caravans and farm machinery. On some open days there is a presentation on how heavy horses were worked on the land. There is a children's play and activity area and a cafe.

www.hillside.org.uk
Sandy Lane, West Runton, NR27 9QH
Open Easter to end October -
closed Saturdays
(and Fridays in April, May, Sept & Oct)
Admission Band C   01603 736200

96 Domestic Animals

Children love to handle small animals and wherever you are in Norfolk and Suffolk there will be somewhere not too far away where they can do this. Many of the places also have sheep, so check out when their lambing season is, as it varies between the various farms.

Church Farm Rare Breeds Centre 97

As it's name indicates many of the animals at Church Farm are rare breeds, such as Bagot and Golden Guernsey goats, Wensleydale and Boreray sheep and Gloucester Old Spot and Kunekune pigs. The information boards are informative, humorous and child friendly. However Church Farm is much more than rare breeds, with a petting pen, tractor and trailer rides, an adventure playground, under cover sand pit and bale climbing area and the very impressive indoor Treetops play area (seen here). There are many special events including lambing from Mid-March to Mid-May.

www.churchfarmstowbardolph.co.uk
Church Farm, Stow Bardolph, PE34 3HT
On the A10 north of Downham Market
Open daily Mid February - end October
Nov - mid Feb - Thurs,Fri,Sat,Sun
01366 382162   Admission Band D

98 Snettisham Farm Park

Snettisham Farm Park is part of a 320 acre working farm. The highlight of the visit for me was a 45 minute ride in a covered trailer to see the herd of more than sixty red deer. As can be seen in the photograph, the deer were not at all shy and the talk by our guide was very informative. In May, June and July you can see deer calves and September is the start of the rutting season. We were there at the time of a school visit, when all the children were able to bottle feed a lamb and collect eggs. Lambing takes place from February to May each year. There is a discovery trail, an adventure playground, a cafe and visitor centre.

www.snettishampark.co.uk
Snettisham Park, Snettisham, PE31 7NQ
Follow signs off A149 - close to church.
Open daily - but call to check winter hours
01485 542425
Admission Band C - Deer safari extra

Gressenhall Farm 99

Gressenhall Farm is at the same location as the workhouse (see page 129) and entry gives access to both. The farm was once used to grow produce for the inmates of the workhouse and is now run as a traditional 1920's farm, with rare breed animals and horses working in the fields. The farmhouse has a traditional range and furniture, a barn houses old farm machinery and in one of the farm buildings is a hands-on display of milking. The grounds include a river valley, water meadows, woodlands, country trails and riverside walks. There are cart rides around the farm and a large adventure play area.

www.museums.norfolk.gov.uk
Gressenhall Farm & Workhouse,
Gressenhall, Dereham, NR20 4DR
Open late March to end October
and usually February half term
01362 880563   Admission Band D

100 Wroxham Barns

The Junior Farm is part of the Wroxham Barns complex which also has a children's funfair (for adults - there are studios, craft shops and a restaurant). Within the farm area there is plenty of hands-on opportunity for children, with feeding sessions every half hour - of rabbits, goats and pigs. When we were there they were bottle feeding lambs. There was also pony grooming and an opportunity to try milking a cow - or at least a good imitation of one. The fun fair area is very popular, with a good selection of rides and activities for younger children.

www.wroxhambarns.co.uk
Wroxham Barns, Tunstead Road, Hoveton NR12 8QU off A1151 north of Wroxham Open daily except 24th, 25th Dec & 1st January - only weekends in January (funfair only at weekends in winter) 01603 783762 Admission to farm Band B

Melsop Farm Park 101

A feature of Melsop Farm Park is the incubation area where children can see the chicks hatching and then handle some of the older chicks. Children are encouraged to interact with all the animals including sheep, goats, pigs and the chickens. There are paddocks for the larger animals and a waterfowl pond. I was particularly attracted to the reindeer and amused by the goat visiting the rabbits in their hutches. There are indoor and outdoor play areas including a covered sandpit, a slide and a trampoline. There is a cafe, with seating that overlooks the indoor play area.

www.melsopfarmpark.co.uk
Ellingham Road, Scoulton NR9 4NT
on the B1108 east of Watton
Open daily in school holidays - otherwise closed on Mondays.
Open w/ends only Jan & Feb up to half term.
01953 851943   Admission Band D

102 Animal Ark

The Animal Ark was previously known as the Norfolk Wildlife Centre. This twenty acre area of parkland has now reincarnated itself by focussing on farm animals and pets which are aimed at younger children. As well as the usual goats, Suffolk sheep, Kunekune pigs, chickens, guinea pigs and donkeys, they have peacocks, chipmunks, terrapins and an aviary of cockatiels. There is an indoor play area for the under sevens and various outdoor play activities, generally aimed at under elevens. There is a cafe and a gift shop.

www.theanimalark.org
Fakenham Road, Gt Witchingham
NR9 5QS 01603 872274
On the A1067 6 miles north west
of Norwich.
Open February half term and from
Easter to October half term
Admission Band D

Aylsham Fun Barn 103

As its name suggests this is an indoor fun barn with additional outdoor activities, including animals to pet and feed. This makes it an excellent destination with young children when the weather is rather variable. The animals include donkeys, horses and lots of goats. There are also chickens running everywhere. The outdoor adventure playground has a wide range of climbing, swinging, crawling and sliding features. One barn has a mountain of woodchips, which children move about with tractors and diggers. The other has all the inflatable bouncy stuff. There is a cafe.

www.aylshamfunbarns.co.uk
Spa Lane, Aylsham NR11 6UE
Just off the A140 Aylsham roundabout
on the B1145 01263 734108
Open daily in school holidays - weekends only in the winter - call or check website for other opening times   Admission Band B

104 Baylham House Farm

Its full title is the Baylham House Rare Breeds Farm and the owners are certainly very committed to breeding endangered farm animals. They are also committed to providing a place where you can experience close contact with livestock and share the enjoyment that a relationship with animals can provide. As can be seen here, the pigs were roaming freely, just waiting to be petted. In the lamb tunnel are six small breeding flocks of rare sheep. Lambing usually takes place in the February half term and the Easter holidays, with shearing usually in the middle of June. There is a cafe.

www.baylham-house-farm.co.uk
Mill Lane, Baylam IP6 8LG 01473 830264
Just off the B1113 mid way between
Needham Market and Great Blakenham.
Open daily from 11am from mid February
to end October Admission Band B

Easton Farm Park 105

Easton Farm Park describes itself as 35 acres of family friendly fun and this is certainly what we saw on our visit. The activities listed on the board on this day included, barrel bug rides, hug a bunny, hold a chick, calf feeding, family train, pony cart rides, egg collecting, pony rides, ferret fun and pig fun. They advise that each child is able to take part in eight activities - included in the entrance price. There is also an indoor soft play area and an outdoor playground, there are walks along the river and of course the pets paddocks. Lambing takes place in March and April. There is a cafe.

www.eastonfarmpark.co.uk
*Easton, Near Wickham Market IP13 0EQ
Off B1078 Signed from the A12
Check - but usually open daily from late
March to mid September, then weekends
then daily in autumn half term, closed in
November 01728 746475 Admission Band E*

106 Suffolk Owl Sanctuary

The Suffolk Owl Sanctuary is a charity established to re-habilitate injured wild birds of prey. It also sets up nest boxes to encourage owls back to the wild. There are over seventy owls and other birds of prey at the sanctuary, many of which participate in the impressive flying demonstrations. These take place up to three times a day from Easter until September. As well as the birds, there are Red Squirrels and chipmunks. There is a woodland walk. Within the Stonham Barns complex are other attractions including cafe, shops, crazy golf and pitch and putt.

www.owl-help.co.uk
Stonham Barns, Pettaugh Road
Stonham Aspal   IP14 6AT
On the A1120 east of A140
Open daily except 25/26 Dec & 1 Jan
01449 711425   Admission by donation -
a guide figure is given.

Pettitts Animal Adventure Park 107

Pettitts Animal Adventure Park could have been included in the theme park section of this book, as the rides probably occupy the same space as the animals and Lily spent more time on the rides than looking at the animals. That's not to say that the animals are not interesting - there are red squirrels, monkeys and parrots and other exotic animals, as well as lots of domestic animals. But the many rides are a great attraction for young children and as they are included in the entry price, Lily was able to ride on every one. There is also a theatre, with three shows a day featuring Bingo the Clown.

www.pettittsadventurepark.co.uk
Church Road, Reedham NR13 3UA
Off the A47 - follow signs from Acle
Open daily from Easter to end October
01493 700094 Admission Band F

108 Pensthorpe

We have already included Pensthorpe in the bird watching section of this book, but the Pensthorpe Conservation Centre is much more than just birds. Pensthorpe is trying to encourage children's love of all wildlife, encouraging close encounters with animals and insects as well as birds. They are clearly succeeding in this objective and undoubtedly this contributed to them being given the EDP Tourism Award for best large visitor attraction in Norfolk in 2009. Their influence has of course gone beyond Norfolk, through their hosting of the BBC Spring Watch programme. To encourage children, Pensthorpe has created a Wildlife Tracker Trail which is both informative and fun. They have placed stamping stations around the reserve for children to stamp the Wild on Wildlife.....

Pensthorpe 109

....booklet which they are given on arrival. The stamping stations are placed at key points such as the pond dipping area.They lead children around the reserve - collecting stamps and collecting facts for their booklet. Once they get all the stamps they receive a free gift. The pictures show the honey bees in the Old School House and the Land Rover and trailer which takes you to the secret parts of the reserve on the Wensum Discovery Tour. The Red Squirrels are part of a breeding programme - they can be seen on a webcam. The fire eater featured in a Mediaeval Spectacular weekend.

www.pensthorpe.com
*Pensthorpe, Fakenham Road, Fakenham
NR21 0LN   01328 851465
On A1067 one mile SE of Fakenham
Open every day except 25/26 December
Admission Band E Discovery tour extra*

110 Theme Parks

We have collectively called these three venues 'Theme Parks' but they are all very different. Without doubt they would each be included in most children's top five days out and so do try and visit them all - even if you have to come back next year!

Pleasurewood Hills Theme Park 111

Pleasurewood Hills is one off the best theme parks in the country and a place that offers an exciting day out for children of all ages. It deservedly won the Suffolk Leisure & Recreation Award in 2009. The rides cater for all ages and physical constitutions, from roller coasters such as the 'Wipeout' shown opposite, which is almost 120' tall and creates over 5G of force, to the sedentary mystery boat ride 'Tales of the Coast'. Two of the other popular rides shown here are the Le Mans race track and Timber Falls, a white water ride. There is a live circus show, sea lion and parrot shows and several cafes.

www.pleasurewoodhills.com
Leisure Way, Corton, NR32 5DZ
SatNav - NR32 4TZ   01502 586000
Open Easter to September in school
holidays and weekends + October half term
Check opening times - Admission Band G

112 BeWILDerwood

The *Daily Telegraph* summed up BeWILDerwood when they wrote - "A 50-acre maze of watery glades, tree houses, ropewalks, and zip wires reached by boat and inhabited by mystical folk. BeWILDerwood is a must see". It is based on the magical children's books written by local author and creator of BeWILDerwood, Tom Blofeld. The *Observer* described it as - "One of the 50 most fabulous things to do in the world". All our grandchildren from Amelia ($1^{1}/_{2}$) to Maisie (12) agree with this - as well as Oscar and his dad - shown here. There is a Snack Shack.

www.bewilderwood.co.uk
Horning Road, Hoveton NR12 8JW
01603 783900   On A1062 between
Wroxham and Horning
Open Feb. half term, Easter to end October
but closed on some Tuesdays and
Wednesdays in April, May, Sept. & Oct.
Check opening times - Admission Band G

Dinosaur Adventure Park

This is one of George and Lily's favourite places, they have been several times but still want to go back. They start with the Dinosaur Trail, looking for dinosaurs in the woods, especially T Rex. They can unearth dinosaur fossils and look for a Lost World Tribe in the Lost World Maze. Within the fun barn there are iguanas, Bearded dragons, millipedes, snakes, cockroaches and other creepy crawlies. Also in the Fun Barn are rabbits and guinea pigs that can be handled. There is a Jurassic putting course and to really burn off energy there is the Raptor Racer pedal car circuit and the adventure play area. There are cafes.

www.dinosauradventure.co.uk
Weston Park, Lenwade NR9 5JW
On the A1067 near Lenwade between
Norwich and Fakenham 01603 876310
Open daily closed only 25/26 December
Check opening times - Admission Band D

114 Land, Sea & Air

It was difficult to think of a simple title to cover this eclectic mix of venues. Many of them are specialised museums, with science and technology featuring in most. They are all extremely interesting, not just for children but probably for most dads as well!

Inspire Discovery Centre 115

I did say that I wouldn't declare a favourite, but if I did then this would be a contender and I know it would be in George and Zak's top three too. The Inspire Discovery Centre is located in a restored medieval church and is a place where children and adults can explore science through hands-on activities. There are over 30 permanent interactive activities based on five themes - forces, light, perception, risk and medieval engineering. They aim at all ages, there are even workshops for under fives on a Sunday morning.There are also half-hour demonstrations such as 'The Really Gross Show'. There is a cafe.

www.inspirediscoverycentre.com
St. Michael's Church, Oak Street, Norwich
NR3 3AE   Open every day
except between Christmas and New Year
Mon-Fri 10am to 4pm Sat-Sun 11am to 5pm
Admission Band C

116 City of Norwich Aviation Museum

This is the place for young aircraft enthusiasts - a museum run by enthusiasts with a collection of more than a dozen historic aircraft. The aircraft include a Harrier, two Hawker Hunters, a Jaguar and a Gloster Meteor. Pride of place is occupied by the Vulcan bomber and on certain days you are allowed to climb up into the cockpit. Other aircraft include a Handley Page Herald and a Westland Whirlwind helicopter. Additionally there are several cockpit sections and parts of planes and other memorabilia in exhibition areas. There is a cafe.

www.cnam.co.uk
Old Norwich Road, Horsham St. Faith, NR10 3JF 01603 893080 Off the A140 on the north side of Norwich Airport April - Oct closed on Mondays, Nov - Mar closed Mon, Tues & Thurs. Usually extended Christmas/New Year closure. Check times & openings before visiting. Admission Band B

Norfolk & Suffolk Aviation Museum 117

It was a great discovery for me to find this large aviation museum tucked away in a quiet part of Suffolk. On the eight acre site they have some sixty aircraft and indoor exhibitions on civil and military aviation in East Anglia. In other buildings there are themed collections for the Royal Observer Corps, RAF Bomber Command, RAF Air-Sea Rescue and others. There are several other specialist exhibitions, including Wartime Childhood Memories. This museum is absolutely packed with artefacts and I will certainly need to go back again. There is a cafe.

www.aviationmuseum.net
Buckeroo Way, The Street, Flixton,
NR35 1NZ 01986 896644 On the B1062
off the A143 two miles west of Bungay.
Open Sun-Thurs Apr to Oct, Tues, Wed &
Sun Nov to Mar. Closed mid Dec-mid Jan
Admission Free (but do donate well)

118 Ipswich Transport Museum

The old trolleybus depot is packed with around 100 exhibits relating to transport in Ipswich. It is the largest collection of transport items in Britain devoted to just one town. Everything was either made or used in and around Ipswich. The range of transport represented is very diverse, from an electric tramcar to a collection of bicycles and from fire engines to prams. Check the website for events and themed open days such as 'Ride a Fire Engine Day' and on another day you can ride on classic buses. The enthusiasts and volunteers here have created a museum of which Ipswich can be proud. There is a cafe.

www.ipswichtransportmuseum.co.uk
Old Trolleybus Depot, Cobham Road,
Ipswich, IP3 9JD 01473 715666
Open - school holidays except Christmas/
New Year. Every Sunday except in
December. Admission Band B

East Anglia Transport Museum 119

The feature of this transport museum is that you can ride on the trams and trolley buses within the grounds of the museum (fares included in the entry price). You can also take a ride on a 2ft gauge railway with diesel locomotives. The street scene has been recreated from the earlier part of the 20th century so that everything appears to be in place, including a shop and car show room. This is another museum created completely by volunteers, who should be congratulated for their achievement.

www.eatm.org.uk
Chapel Road, Carlton Colville, NR33 8BL
01502 518459 Situated 3 miles SW of Lowestoft just off A146. Open Sundays and Thursdays April - September   Sun 11 - 5pm Thurs 2 - 5pm Open every day in summer holidays (except Mondays) and Easter week + some extra Saturdays in April - September Open Bank Holidays Check on website or call   Admission Band D

120 RAF Air Defence Radar Museum

This is a remarkable museum. Neatishead was the centre of 'Cold War' operations for the UK up to 2004 and here you can sit at the controls of the actual radars in the operations room where they monitored USSR activity up to 1993. As well as all the original equipment from this period, they have recreated the development and use of radar through the Second World War. A third area entitled 'From Home Defence to Space Defence' brings the technology up to date. You can browse around the museum, but we recommend that you take a guided tour with the knowledgeable ex RAF volunteers.

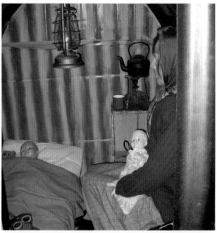

www.radarmuseum.co.uk
Neatishead, NR12 8YB   01692 631485
North of the A1062 east from Wroxham - near Horning Open Apr - Oct on Tues, Thurs & second Sat in month. Winter open second Sat only   Admission Band C

Radio Museum at Muckleburgh 121

This radio museum, which is housed in a hut at the Muckleburgh Collection, (see over) is run by the North Norfolk Amateur Radio Group. They have built up a unique collection, dating back to the early days of radio and incorporating military communication equipment. Here George is being taught to send his name in Morse code and later sitting at their impressive amateur radio station G6HL. Children are always fascinated by the potato powered radio, as well as hearing the last messages from the Titanic. The knowledgeable volunteers are happy to talk about the exhibits and about the hobby of amateur radio.

www.gb2mc.co.uk
Muckleburgh Collection, Weybourne NR25 7EG On A149 west of Sheringham Open - Wed's & Thurs 10 - 4pm, Sundays 1 - 4pm (Easter to end October) . Admission Free - do give a donation.

122 Muckleburgh Collection

The Muckleburgh Collection is claimed to be the UK's largest privately owned working military museum, with over 120 tanks, guns and vehicles, as well as thousands of other artefacts. There are a number of tanks, including a Sherman and a Chieftain, which are used to give working demonstrations. A US personnel carrier, the 'Gamma Goat', gives hair raising rides along the coast. Other exhibits include historic memorabilia from the Suffolk and Norfolk Yeomanry, RAF Reconnaissance, Air Sea Rescue, and a unique collection of naval and civilian model ships. There is a play and picnic area and a cafe.

www.muckleburgh.co.uk
Muckleburgh Collection, Weybourne NR25 7EG 01263 588210 On A149 west of Sheringham Open - every day Easter to end October & February half term. Weekends in March . Admission Band D

Thursford Collection 123

The Thursford Collection is claimed to be the world's largest collection of steam engines and organs. Live organ shows are given twice a day. Also within the large museum building are three impressive hundred year old classic fairground rides, restored to working order. One is a three abreast set of 1896 Savages' Gallopers and another is a Savages' Venetian Gondola Switchback Ride. Thursford is the home of the famous Christmas Spectacular and Santa's Magical Journey. Behind the scenes tours are given through the summer (at extra cost). There is a playground and a cafe.

www.thursford.com
Thursford Green, Thursford, NR21 0AS 01328 878477 Off the A148 between Holt & Fakenham Open Easter to end September 12 - 5 pm closed on Saturdays except Easter Saturday. Admission Band D.

124 Strumpshaw Steam Museum

Strumpshaw is an undercover steam museum, a small rare breeds centre, a narrow gauge railway and a countryside walk. The museum has steam engines and lorries, working mechanical organs, a 100 ton working beam engine, and an Art Deco 1930's cinema organ. The Strumpshaw Steam Museum hosts a steam engine rally over the Bank Holiday weekend at the end of May. As well as visiting steam engines, there are traditional fairground rides and vintage and classic cars. There is a cafe and a picnic area.

www.strumpshawsteammuseum.co.uk
Strumpshaw, Norwich NR13 4HR
01603 714535 South of the A47 between Norwich & Acle. Open Easter week & early May Bank Holiday week. Sundays, Wednesdays and Bank Holidays to end June then daily (except Saturdays) to beginning of October   Admission Band B

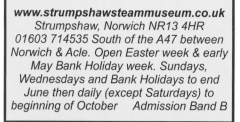

Long Shop Museum 125

The Long Shop Museum shows the history of Garretts, a family owned engineering company that occupied a large factory site in Leiston for over 200 years, until its final closure in 1980. The Long Shop is the last original part of the factory and it was where they manufactured steam engines. Over its time the company manufactured a wide range of products, including parts for steam locomotives, aeroplanes, weapons, trolley buses and toys. The Garrett story reflects much of the history of British manufacturing. Displays also provide information about the nearby Sizewell nuclear power station.

www.longshop.care4free.net
Main Street Leiston IP16 4ES
01728 832189 Generally opens every day from just before Easter to end October Check website for free open day and steam days   Admission Band B

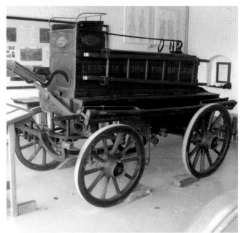

126 Lowestoft Maritime Museum

The Lowestoft Maritime Museum is another excellent museum created and run entirely by volunteers. The Lowestoft & East Suffolk Maritime Society established it in 1968, since when it has been extended several times including a doubling in size in 2009. The museum covers the history of fishing and of Lowestoft, one of the UK's leading fishing ports, as well as a centre for shipbuilding. The museum has reconstructed life on a fishing boat, with the diorama shown below and also a reconstructed wheelhouse. It has an excellent display of model ships and many other maritime artefacts.

www.lowestoftmaritimemuseum.org.uk
Sparrow's Nest Park. Whapload Road,
Lowestoft NR32 1XG 01502 561963
Usually open daily from May to October
- check if open before May
Admission Band A

RNLI Henry Blogg Museum

When you are in Cromer you must visit the RNLI museum, named after the RNLI's most decorated lifeboatman. He served for 53 years (saving 873 lives) and was coxswain of the Cromer Lifeboat for 38 years, until he retired in 1947 at the age of 71. He died in 1954. There are many interactive displays to interest children, with the opportunity for them to try on kit, practice Morse code, send messages with flags, and meet Henry Blogg and his dog. The centrepiece of the museum is the Watson Class lifeboat HF Bailey, which was Blogg's lifeboat in World War II.

www.rnli.org.uk
The Rocket House, The Gangway, Cromer
NR27 9ET 01263 511294
The museum directly faces Cromer's East Beach.   Opens all year but generally closes on a Monday - check times.
Admission Free - but do donate generously

"Children who visit museums get better grades at school"
- is a finding of research from the University of Leicester.
We have selected some of the best museums in our region
for inclusion here - not just because of their educational
value. Today many museums are genuinely interesting
and fun for children. They can also be thought provoking,
as was the Gressenhall Workhouse (depicted here) for
George and Lily.

Gressenhall Workhouse 129

A visit to Gressenhall Workhouse should be on everyone's agenda. The buildings here functioned as a workhouse for 170 years and the story told by the rooms that have been created as the Workhouse Experience is a compelling one. Other parts of the building house displays on village life and farming. One room has been furnished as in the 1950's. The Village Row is a recreation of a village street, complete with seed merchants, grocery shop, blacksmith, garage, post office and the village schoolroom, where children can take part in a lesson. Entry also covers the farm (see page 99).

www.museums.norfolk.gov.uk
Gressenhall Farm & Workhouse,
Gressenhall, Dereham, NR20 4DR
Open late March to end October
and usually February half term
01362 880563   Admission Band D

130 Norwich Castle

We often have a problem in illustrating a venue with just four photographs and this is particularly so with Norwich Castle. As there is so much to see and do, we have allocated two pages. It was built by the Normans 900 years ago and today it is both a fine example of a castle and Norfolk's principle museum. Children can find out what life was like in the Norman keep through touch screens and computer animation and they are usually fascinated by the garderobes (4 berth toilets). Working models show how the Castle was built, how the stone was transported from Caen in Normandy. Another area is given to the story of East Anglia's Queen Boudicca and a favourite here is a chariot with video projection, depicting what it was like to go into battle against the Romans.

Norwich Castle 131

In the Anglo-Saxon and Viking Gallery children can find out what life was like in East Anglia after the Romans left. Here there is a reconstruction of an Anglo-Saxon grave site. Early Egyptian history is covered with a tomb and mummies, which have their own particular fascination. There are guided tours of the battlements and dungeons - although there are minimum age requirements (Battlements 8, dungeons age 5). Another favourite area with the children is the natural history gallery. There are organised activities for children during every holiday, including George's favourite - Medieval Mayhem. There is a cafe.

www.museums.norfolk.gov.uk
Castle Meadow, Norwich, NR1 3JU
Open daily except 24-27 December
& 1 January (Sundays 1-5pm)
01603 493625 Admission Band C

132 Tide & Time Museum

This excellent museum in Great Yarmouth has won many awards and has been a finalist in others, including both Gulbenkian and European Museum of the Year and so it goes without saying that it should be included on your must visit list. The museum is about the history of Great Yarmouth, in particular its maritime and fishing heritage. They have recreated the Victorian 'Row' allowing you to see inside a fisherman's home. They also depict the quayside as it was in the 1950's, the wheelhouse of a drifter and a herring smoke house. Another area of the museum shows life in Great Yarmouth in World War II.

www.museums.norfolk.gov.uk
Blackfriars Road, Gt. Yarmouth NR30 3BX
Open every day (Except usually 24,25,26 December and 1st January) - check times
01493 743930   Admission Band C

Cromer Museum 133

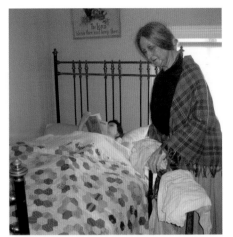

The centrepiece of this museum is an actual fisherman's cottage, which has been furnished to show how life was in the 19th century. Children can dress up in Victorian clothes to see what they would have looked like in these times. In the new geology gallery there is a collection of fossils, all which have been found in Norfolk. There are displays about the West Runton Elephant, Britain's oldest and most complete elephant fossil (see also page 37). Other displays relate to early man in Norfolk showing flint arrowheads and axes. Events are organised for children in the Easter and summer holidays.

www.museums.norfolk.gov.uk
East Cottages, Church Street, NR27 9HB
(Next to the church) Open daily 1 March to
31 October, closed on Sundays in
winter, check times.
01263 513543   Admission Band A

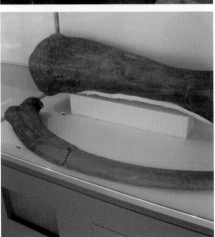

134 Sutton Hoo

Sutton Hoo has been described by the National Trust as one of Britain's most important and atmospheric archaeological sites. A 90 foot long Anglo-Saxon burial ship was discovered in 1939 and this led to the discovery of the most amazing collection of treasures that had lain undisturbed within the ship for over 1300 years. A replica of the famous helmet is displayed in the visitor centre, where there is also a superb full sized reconstruction of the burial chamber found in the ship, with the treasures laid out. There are guided tours of the burial mounds.

www.nationaltrust.org.uk
Tranmer House, Sutton Hoo, Woodbridge, IP12 3DJ East of Woodbridge A1152 then B1083, 01394 389700 Generally open daily in school holidays, otherwise Wed-Sun or weekends only Nov-Feb, check times. Admission Band C (Free for NT members)

West Stow Anglo Saxon Village 135

This reconstructed Anglo Saxon Village is within West Stow Country Park, along with a visitor centre and Anglo-Saxon museum. It is known that this site has been occupied by a succession of peoples since c5000 BC with Anglo-Saxon settlers arriving around 420 AD. The reconstructed houses have been built with different techniques, using tools that would have been available. This has tested out ideas about how things might have been done at that time. Your visit to the Anglo-Saxon village can be combined with the walks and nature trails of the country park.

www.stedmundsbury.gov.uk
West Stow Country Park, Icklingham Road, West Stow, IP28 6HG Off A1101 between Bury St. Edmunds and Mildenhall. Open daily except for Christmas/ New Year period - check for this and opening times. 01284 728718   Admission Band C

136 Town House Museum of Lynn Life

The Town House Museum depicts the history and domestic life in King's Lynn from Medieval times to the 1950's. In the 17th century room is a reconstructed fireplace, with objects showing what life was like for those living through the siege of Lynn during the Civil War. There is a Victorian child's nursery with a doll's house and toys of the period. The Victorian kitchen has everyday items used by the servants and the cook. A display of home life during the world wars shows the difficult times endured by the people of King's Lynn. The 1950's room allows us to tell our grandchildren what it was like to grow up at this time.

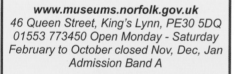

www.museums.norfolk.gov.uk
46 Queen Street, King's Lynn, PE30 5DQ
01553 773450 Open Monday - Saturday
February to October closed Nov, Dec, Jan
Admission Band A

Museum of East Anglian Life 137

This museum was a complete surprise, being in the centre of Stowmarket I was only expecting a single building with artefacts, not an eighty acre park with numerous buildings, a farm area and woodland and riverside nature trails. Some of the buildings house the displays of East Anglian life and others are restored historic buildings, such as a water mill and a Victorian tin tabernacle. Other displays relate to the trades and crafts of the past, including charcoal maker, hurdle maker, smithy, cooper and rope making. You must visit this award winning museum. There is a cafe.

www.eastanglianlife.org.uk
Iliffe Way, Stowmarket IP14 1DL
In the centre of Stowmarket next to the ASDA supermarket. 01449 612229
Generally open daily from end March to end October - check dates & times
Admission Band D

138 Yesterday's World Exhibition

Yesterday's World is situated on Great Yarmouth's Golden Mile and describes itself as "A Spectacular Time Travel Adventure". They claim to have used over 150,000 artefacts from the reign of Queen Victoria to the 1960's to bring to life a recreation of 'yesteryear'. The recreations include an ironmonger's shop, a 19th century apothecary, a toy shop, a car mechanic's garage and a railway station. There are dioramas depicting Queen Victoria, Frankenstein, Jekyll & Hyde and HG Wells' Time Machine. A ride on an original renovated 1898 3-abreast galloper carousel is included in the ticket price. There is a Victorian tearoom.

www.yesterdaysworld.co.uk
34 Marine Parade, Great Yarmouth
NR30 2EN 01493 331148
Open daily 1st March - 23rd December
Admission Band E

Dragon Hall 139

Dragon Hall is a Grade 1 listed trading hall built in about 1430. It is a unique legacy of medieval life and is one of the most important historic buildings in Norfolk. Dragon Hall was not a home but the magnificent first-floor Great Hall was the showroom of a late medieval merchant called Robert Toppes. It is stated that - "Learning is at the heart of Dragon Halls vision, come to us to find out about the past and learn to look at the present". There are interactive displays, models, cloths to dress up in and family packs are available. There is a range of organised craft and art activities during the school holidays.

www.dragonhall.org
115-123 King Street, Norwich, NR1 1QE
10 minute walk from the city centre.
Open March - October, Monday to Friday
and Sunday afternoon - check times
01603 663922 Admission Band B

140 Ancient House Museum

The Ancient House Museum of Thetford Life is what its name describes. Set in a beautiful crooked Tudor house it tells the story of Thetford and the Brecks. One thousand years ago Thetford was one of the largest towns in England and the Vikings attacked it three times, but despite this the museum shows that the town flourished through this period. The museum tells the story of people who had previously lived in the house and what life would have been like for them. This includes the Newton family and their lodgers who appeared in the 1901 census. Hands on activities are organised for children and families, taking place throughout the year.

www.museums.norfolk.gov.uk
*21-23 White Hart Street, Thetford, IP24 1AA
Open Monday - Saturday, closed 24 -28
December & 1st January - check times
01842 752599 Admission Band A*

Nelson Museum 141

This museum celebrates the life of Norfolk's famous naval hero and does it superbly within a Georgian Merchant's house. Through hands-on activities you can explore Nelson's career, from his Norfolk childhood through his famous battles, to his tragic heroic death. Children can try a hammock, play ship's games and examine cannons from Nelson's time. A new exhibition examines - through strategy games and battle analysis - why Nelson was such a good leader and motivator of his men. Family activity days are organised through the year, such as a Pirate Day and 'Gruesome Georgians'.

www.nelson-museum.co.uk
26 South Quay, Gt. Yarmouth, NR30 2RG
Open daily except Saturdays (1-4pm on Sundays) usually closed December and New Year - check dates/times
01493 850698 Admission Band A

142 Elizabethan House

The splendid Elizabethan House on Great Yarmouth's South Quay, depicts the lives of the families who lived in it from Tudor to Victorian times. The dining room takes visitors back to the 1590's, when the house was owned by a Benjamin Cooper and when children had to stand at the table (smaller ones on a stool). John Carter the owner of the house in 1648, together with his great friend Oliver Cromwell and others, plotted the death of Charles I in the 'Conspiracy Room'. There is a Tudor bedroom and Victorian parlour and kitchen. Old toys can be seen in the toy room with replicas to play with.

www.museums.norfolk.gov.uk
4 South Quay, Gt. Yarmouth, NR30 2QH
Generally open daily April to end October
(12-4pm Sat & Sun) - check dates/times
01493 855746 Admission Band A
(Free entry to National Trust members)

Lynn Museum 143

The Lynn Museum is home to Seahenge, the Bronze age timber circle discovered further along the Norfolk coast at Holme-next-the-Sea in 1998. Within the museum is a life size replica of Seahenge and also around half of the 55 original 4000 year old timbers, in a setting that reflects the place in which they were originally found. The museum covers a wide range of local history, from a hoard of Iron Age gold coins found locally, to local manufacturing companies. These include Dodman's Engineers and Savages, a famous manufacturer of fairground machinery, carousels and gallopers.

www.museums.norfolk.gov.uk
*Market Street, King's Lynn, PE30 1NL
Open Tuesday - Saturday, closed 24 -28
December & 1st January - check times
01553 775001 Admission Band A
Check free admission in winter*

144 The Tolhouse

This museum which is primarily about the history of crime and punishment in Great Yarmouth, is based in a 12th Century former merchant's house and takes in the only surviving part of Yarmouth prison. The audio guide allows you to hear the gaoler and his prisoners describe their experiences. You discover the fate of thieves, smugglers, witches, pirates and murderers. In the very oldest part of the prison where the poorest people were imprisoned, you meet the two characters Charles Girdlestone and Sarah Hunnibal. In contrast there is a reproduction of a modern prison cell.

www.museums.norfolk.gov.uk
Tolhouse Street, Gt. Yarmouth, NR30 2SH
Situated behind the library
Open daily April to end October
(12-4pm Sat & Sun) - check dates/times
01493 745526 Admission Band A

Swaffham Museum 145

Swaffham Museum is an excellent example of a small independent museum run by volunteers and deserving of our support. It is housed in a Grade II listed town house that has also been the Town Hall and is now home to a collection of local artefacts which span from prehistoric times to the present day. The Egyptian Gallery shows how local Swaffham man Howard Carter discovered the tomb of Tutankhamun. The Archaeology Room has fossils, Roman sandals, and coins discovered in nearby fields. When we visited there was an interesting exhibition entitled 'Memories of Swaffham's War'.

www.swaffhammuseum.co.uk
4 London Street, Swaffham, PE37 4DQ
Open end March to 23 December Tuesday to Saturday & Bank Holidays - check times
01760 721230   Admission Band A

146 Toad Hole Cottage Museum

This small cottage on the How Hill Nature Reserve (see page 51) shows what life was like on the marshes about 100 years ago. Marshmen worked harvesting the reed and sedge, catching fish and eels, shooting wildfowl, cutting the marsh hay, looking after cattle and attending to the drainage mills on the marshes. The kitchen or living room was the main focus of home life, with not too much in the way of convenience or comfort. Cooking was done on the range using peat for fuel. There was no running water and candles or rush lights were used for lighting. In the larder you can see the store of preserved food.

www.broads-authority.gov.uk
Toad Hole Cottage, How Hill
North of the A1062 at Ludham
Open daily Easter to end October
- check times
01692 678763 Admission Free

The objective of the Museum of the Broads is for you to enter the world of broads, marshes, mills, reeds, wildlife and marshmen. To discover how man helped forge this unique landscape, from medieval peat diggers to the holiday maker of today. There are broads boats from the last two centuries and a Victorian steam launch usually operates on Tuesdays, Wednesdays and Thursdays. There are instructive displays, such as this one showing how pulleys lighten loads and the one below it explains about gears and cogs. This is another excellent museum run by local volunteers and worthy of support.

www.museumofthebroads.org
The Staithe, Stalham NR12 9DA
South of the A149
Open daily just before Easter to
end October check times
01692 581681 Admission Band B

148 Ipswich Museum

I was very impressed with Ipswich Museum and I was pleased to find that entry is free. This meant that the museum was very busy, with many families making return visits. Visitors first see a huge woolly mammoth as they enter the museum, along with other animals in the Natural History Gallery. The story of Queen Boudicca and the Iceni tribe is well presented and of course very relevant to Norfolk and Suffolk. There is a very good Egyptian gallery with interactive games and puzzles. Other displays relate to the Anglo-Saxon origins of Ipswich and to World War II in Ipswich.

www.ipswich.gov.uk
High Street, Ipswich, IP1 3QH
Five minutes walk from the town centre
Open to Saturday - 10 to 5pm
Check Christmas/New Year closures
01473 433550 Admission Free

As their website says - "The local history collection here is an intriguing mixture of the humdrum and the bizarre, the mundane and the macabre..". One area of the museum deals with childhood. There is a beautifully furnished dolls' house from 1871, a collection of dolls and also a collection of teddy bears. On the macabre side is a 19th century child's bier, used to carry the coffins of children to their funerals. You can download children's quiz sheets from the website prior to your visit. There are frequent organised events and meetings of the Bury Young Archaeologists club (for 8 to 16 year olds).

www.moyseshall.org
Cornhill, Bury St Edmunds IP33 1DX
Open daily - closed Bank Holidays and between Christmas and New Year
01284 706183 Admission Band B

150 Bircham Windmill

Windmills and other mills are an important part of our heritage and are educationally valuable places to take children, as they show both how food is produced and also the use of gears and mechanisms. There are several windmills across the two counties which are open to the public, but we have chosen to feature the windmill at Bircham. It is open daily in the season and has other activities such as sheep milking which takes place every day at 2pm. Bircham Windmill won the EDP Tourism in Norfolk award for the best small visitor attraction in 2009. Check their website for special events.

www.birchamwindmill.co.uk
Great Bircham, PE31 6SJ, 01485 578393
On B1153 off A148 Six miles east of
Sandringham, Open daily from Easter to
end September. Admission Band B

Letheringsett Watermill 151

At the time of the Domesday Book there were 580 water mills including one at Letheringsett, interestingly there were no windmills at this time. The present mill at Letheringsett was built in 1802 and after falling into disrepair has been restored by the present miller Mike Thurlow. It is now the last working water powered flour mill in Norfolk, producing a very fine grade of flour from locally grown wheat. Mike holds regular working demonstrations of milling and gives a tour of the mill on most weekday afternoons, giving an informative and fascinating insight into the mill.

www.letheringsettwatermill.co.uk
Riverside Road, Letheringsett NR25 7YD
Off the A148, one mile west of Holt
Closed Sundays, Bank holidays and some
days over Christmas - mill usually
working Tues - Fri pm from May to Sept
Check winter working 01263 713153

152 Woodbridge Tide Mill

A tide mill uses trapped tidal water to turn the machinery. When the tide comes in it flows into a mill pond and when it goes out the water is released to flow under the water wheel and turn the machinery. There has been a tide mill on this site since 1170, the present building dates from 1793. You can view the mill on three floors, where you will see the machinery and information.

www.woodbridgesuffolk.info
Located on Tide Mill Way off Quayside
Usually open Sat to Mon at Easter,
weekends in Apr & Oct. Every day 1 May to
30 September. 11.00 to 5.00 pm. Check info
with the Tourist Information Centre
01473 384880   Admission Band A

Pakenham Watermill

This is the last working water mill in Suffolk. Milling demonstrations usually take place on the first Thursday morning of each month. At other times you can have a guided tour of the mill to find out how it works and learn about traditional wholemeal flour. There is a picturesque mill pond and garden and a tearoom selling homemade cakes. There are various organised events - see website.

www.pakenhamwatermill.co.uk
Mill Road, Pakenham, IP31 2NB
Off A143 7 miles east of Bury St Edmunds
Generally open Thursdays, Saturdays,
Sundays & Bank Holidays from Easter to
end October 01284 724075
Admission Band A

Fisherman's Heritage Centre 153

This centre which is housed in an old fishing shed is dedicated to the privately operated lifeboats that supported the fishermen of Sheringham until 1935. The last of these, the Henry Ramey Upcher, is on display.

www.sheringham-preservation.org.uk
Westcliff Sheringham
Open Easter to end September, Wednesday to Friday 12 to 4pm also Tues & Sat in peak times.
. Admission Free but do give a donation

True's Yard Museum

True's Yard is all that remains of King's Lynn's old fishing community known as the North End. There are two remaining fisherman's cottages which have original furniture and other artefacts that show what life was like for the families who lived here. At one time a family of eleven lived in one of the cottages, with all nine children sleeping in the one and only bed. A fishing smack built in 1904 is located in the yard behind the cottages. This is a most delightful small museum.

Unfortunately we were not given permission to reproduce internal photographs of the cottages.

www.truesyard.co.uk
North Street, King's Lynn
PE30 1QW   01553 770479
Open Tuesdays to Saturdays
Open all year except
Christmas - New Year
Admission Band A

154 Southwold Lighthouse

Lighthouses are fascinating places to visit and educational from a number of aspects. We are fortunate in having two working lighthouses in our region. This one is located near the centre of Southwold, it is a coastal mark for passing shipping and guides vessels into Southwold harbour. The tour of the lighthouse lasts for approximately twenty minutes and children must be at least one metre tall.

www.trinityhouse.co.uk
Stradbroke Road, Southwold 01502 722576
Usually open Wed - Sun in peak summer
See website or notice on entrance gate for
full list of openings. Admission Band B

Happisburgh Lighthouse

Happisburgh is the only lighthouse in the UK to be independently run. After threat of closure by Trinity House in 1988 it was saved by the local community. The lighthouse was repainted in 1990 during the filming of the BBC programme 'Challenge Anneka'. Children under the age of eight are not allowed to climb the 112 steps to the lantern.

www.happisburgh.org/lighthouse
Located just to the south east of
Happisburgh village
Usually open Easter Sunday & Monday,
Spring & August Bank Holidays and
Sundays in the school summer holidays.
Admission Band A

In our two counties we are fortunate in having three historic castles and a fort, all under the jurisdiction of English Heritage. Orford Castle is one of England's most complete and unusual keeps. Castle Rising is one of the largest and best preserved keeps in England. Framlingham Castle is a magnificent example of a late 12th century castle. Landguard is a spectacular coastal artillery fort built in the 18th century with additions in both the 19th and 20th centuries - and in use until 1956.

www.english-heritage.org.uk

Orford Castle *IP12 2ND in Orford on B1084 Admission Band B*
Castle Rising *PE31 6AH 4 miles NE of King's Lynn off A149   Admission Band B*
Framlingham Castle *IP13 9BP in Framlingham on B1116. Admission Band C*
Landguard Fort *IP11 3TX 1 mile south of Felixstowe town centre. Admission Band A*

All he could do was, "Quack, Quack, Q

156 Additional Information

Admission price bands

As a guide we have shown price bands that represent the combined admission cost of one adult plus one child. Often young children are free and usually a lower family rate is available for two adults plus two children. Check venue websites for exact prices and available offers.

Band	Price range		Band	Price range
A	under £4.99		D	£10.00 - £12.99
B	£5.00 - £7.99		E	£13.00 - £15.99
C	£8.00 - £9.99		F	£16.00 - £19.99
			G	£20.00 +

Contact information

Norfolk Wildlife Trust - www.norfolkwildlifetrust.org.uk
Bewick House, 22 Thorpe Road, Norwich,
NR1 1RY 01603 625540

Suffolk Wildlife Trust - www.suffolkwildlife.co.uk
Carlton Marshes - NR33 8HU 01502 564250
Lackford Lakes - IP28 6HX 01284 728706
Redgrave & Lopham Fen - IP22 2HX
01379 688333

RSPB - www.rspb.org.uk
Titchwell Marsh - 01485 210779
Minsmere - 01728 648281
Lakenheath Fen - 01842 863400
Strumpshaw Fen - 01603 715191

Pensthorpe - www.pensthorpe.com 01328 851465
Fakenham Road, Fakenham NR21 0LN
01328 851465

National Trust - www.nationaltrust.org.uk 0844 800 1895

157 Additional Information

Canoe hire on the Broads

www.thecanoeman.com

(trips available with camping included) - 01603 499177

Bungay - Outney Meadow Caravan Park 01986 892338

Burgh St. Peter - Waveney River Centre 01502 677343

Geldeston - Rowancraft 01508 518208

Salhouse Broad - 07795 145475 or 01603 722775

Sutton Staithe Boatyard - 01692 581653

Wayford Bridge - Bank Dayboats 01692 582457

Wroxham - Barnes Brinkcraft 01603 782625

Martham - Martham Boats 01493 740249

Hickling - Whispering Reeds 01692 598314

Day boats on the Broads

Most of the above boatyards hire day boats and a
selection of the many others include -

Hoveton - Barnes Brinkcraft 01603 782625

Wroxham - Broads Tours 01603 782207

Ludham Bridge - Ludham Bridge Boatyard 01692 631011

Potter Heigham - Herbert Woods 01692 670711

Martham - Martham Boats 01493 740249

Brundall - Fencraft 01603 715011

Loddon - Pacific Cruisers 01508 520321

Beccles - CC Marine 01502 713703

Oulton Broad Day Boats 01502 589556

Sailing boats on the Broads

Places where you can hire sailing boats include -

Ludham - Hunter's Yard 01692 678263

Upton - Eastwood Whelpton 01493 750430

Horning - Norfolk Broads Yachting Co. 01692 631330

For more extensive lists of boatyards see the Broads
Authority website -**www.broads-authority.gov.uk**

158 Additional Information

Cycle Hire

A selection of the many places from where you can hire bikes -

Hoveton/Horning - Broadland Cycle Hire (in the car park at BeWILDerwood) 07887 480331 www.broadlandcyclehire.co.uk

Bungay - Outney Meadow Caravan Park 01986 892338
www.outneymeadow.co.uk

Burgh St. Peter - Waveney River Centre 01502 677343
www.waveneyrivercentre.co.uk

Clippesby - Clippesby Hall 01493 367800 www.clippesby.com

Thetford Forest - Bike-Art 01842 810090 www.bike-art.com

Kelling Heath - Huff & Puff Cycles 07788 132909
www.cyclenorfolk.co.uk

Sheringham - The Bike Shed 01263 822255
www.thebikeshed.biz

Ipswich - Alton Cycle Hire 01473 328873
www.altoncyclehire.co.uk

Darsham - Byways Bicycles 01728 668764
www.bywaysbicycles.co.uk

Bircham Windmill - 01485 578393
www.birchamwindmill.co.uk

Blakeney Point seal trips

Bean's Boats - 01263 740505 www.beansboattrips.co.uk

Temples - 01263 740791 www.sealtrips.co.uk

Bishop's Boats - 01263 740753 www.norfolksealtrips.co.uk

Beach safety and safe beach information

www.rnli.org.uk/beachsafety

www.goodbeachguide.co.uk

www.blueflag.org.uk

www.nationalbeachsafety.org.uk

159 Additional Information

Information Centres

Broads Authority

Beccles - 01502 713196

Hoveton/Wroxham - 01603 782281

How Hill - 01692 678763

Potter Heigham - 01692 677016

Ranworth - 01603 270453

Whitlingham - 01603 617332

Tourist Information Centres

Norfolk

Attleborough - 01953 456930

Aylsham - 01263 733903

Burnham Deepdale -

01485 210256

Cromer - 0871 200 3071

Dereham - 01362 698992

Diss - 01379 650523

Downham Market - 01366 383287

Great Yarmouth - 01493 846346

Harleston - 01379 851917

Holt - 0871 200 3071

Hunstanton - 01485 532610

King's Lynn - 01553 763044

Loddon - 01508 521028

Mundesley - 01263 721070

Norwich - 01603 213999

Sheringham - 0871 200 3071

Stalham - 01692 581681

Swaffham - 01760 722255

Thetford - 01842 751975

Walsingham - 01328 820510

Watton - 01953 880212

Wells-next-the-Sea -

0871 200 3071

Wymondham - 01953 604721

Suffolk

Aldeburgh - 01728 453637

Beccles - 01502 713196

Bury St Edmunds -

01284 764667

Felixstowe - 01394 276770

Flatford - 01206 299460

Ipswich - 01473 258070

Lavenham - 01787 248207

Lowestoft - 01502 533600

Newmarket - 01638 667200

Southwold - 01502 724729

Stowmarket - 01449 676800

Sudbury - 01787 881320

Woodbridge - 01394 382240

Acknowledgements

We would like to thank the following organisations for allowing us to reproduce the photographs that we took and for providing the venues that give children so much enjoyment. British Crabbing Federation, Pedlar's Barrow Puppet School, Norwich Puppet Theatre, Hilltop Outdoor Centre, Kelling Heath Holiday Park, Forestry Commission, Adventure Forest Ltd, RNLI, The Glide Surf School, Danny and the Little Gems Rock Shop, The Wizard Maze, Southwold Maze, Priory Maze, Norfolk Ski Club, Glandford Shell Museum, Sheringham & District Preservation Society, Wildfowl & Wetlands Trust, Norfolk Wildlife Trust, Suffolk Wildlife Trust, RSPB, Pensthorpe, Broads Authority, Suffolk County Council, St. Edmundsbury Borough Council, Mid Suffolk District Council, Norfolk County Council, North Norfolk District Council, Fairhaven Garden Trust, Salhouse Broad, Whitlingham Charitable Trust, Holkham Estate, North Norfolk Railway, Wells & Walsingham Railway, Bure Valley Railway, Mid-Norfolk Railway, Mid-Suffolk Railway, Wells Harbour Railway, Bressingham Museum & Gardens, Banham Zoo, Africa Alive, Thrigby Hall Wildlife Gardens, Amazona Zoo, Oasis Camel Centre, Redwings Horse Sanctuary, World Horse Welfare, Hillside Animal Sanctuary, Church Farm Rare Breeds Centre, Snettisham Farm Park, Norfolk Museums & Archaeology Service, Wroxham Barns, Melsop Farm Park, Animal Ark, Aylsham Fun Barn, Baylham House Farm, Easton Farm Park, Suffolk Owl Sanctuary, Pettitts Animal Adventure Park, Pleasurewood Hills, BeWILDerwood, Dinosaur Adventure Park, Inspire Discovery Centre, City of Norwich Aviation Museum, Norfolk & Suffolk Aviation Museum, Ipswich Transport Museum, East Anglia Transport Museum, RAF Air Defence Radar Museum, North Norfolk Amateur Radio Group, Muckleborough Collection, Thursford Collection, Long Shop Museum, Strumpshaw Steam Museum, Lowestoft Maritime Museum, RNLI Henry Blogg Museum, West Stow Anglo Village Trust, Museum of East Anglia Life, Yesterday's World, Dragon Hall, The Norfolk & Norwich Heritage Trust, Nelson Museum, Swaffham Museum, Museum of the Broads, Bircham Windmill, Letheringsett Watermill, Woodbridge Tide Mill, Pakenham Watermill, True's Yard Museum, Trinity House, Happisburgh Lighthouse, English Heritage, Colchester & Ipswich Museum Service, Borough Council of King's Lynn & West Norfolk, and last but not least - Will Appleyard for his underwater photographs.